He sent **His**

Word *and*

He **Healed**

Me *Psalm 107:20*

A remarkable story of hope and healing

Jacquelin Priestley

His Word Healed Me

A remarkable story of hope and healing

Published by ABM Publications
©2014 by Jacquelin Priestley
ISBN: 978-1-931820-20-2

If you would like to order more books, please contact us at
www.HisWordHealedMe.com

Formatting & Editing: Sherry Ward and Jacquelin Priestley
Book Design: Andi Watari (andi.watari@gmail.com)
Book cover photo: Jacquelin Priestley
Headshot & Makeup: Romaine Markus of London
Website Design: Allyson Gideon
Printed in United States of America

<u>DEDICATION</u>

This book is dedicated to the One Who holds
my life and times in His hands,
The one true Living Lord,
Who came to bring us the news that we are loved.
John 1:1, 4, 14

    *   *   *

Sing to the Lord; bless His Name,

Each day proclaim the good news that He saves!

Publish His glorious deeds among the nations.

Tell everyone about the amazing things He does.

Psalm 96:2-3 (NLT)

Foreward

There are exciting updates since **His Word Healed Me** was first released in April 2010 –

Two months after going to press, **His Word Healed Me** was highlighted in a message by Senior Pastor Bayless Conley of Cottonwood Church in Southern California. He was teaching about tenacity of faith and mentioned my story, saying it illustrates in detail how to apply God's Word on a practical level in difficult circumstances. He highly recommended **His Word Healed Me** as a "great read with quite an impact!"

His wife, Pastor Janet Conley, said the book powerfully touched her heart and provided fresh insights she'd never had before about how alive God's Word really is!

Consistent comments have been that the book is very relatable, "a real page turner" and an easy read, yet offers great depth.

Emails are coming in: two people have written about being healed while reading the book! Others tell of growth in their faith and wonderful prayer results: a woman named Shirley was losing leg strength, fearful of needing a wheelchair due to Multiple Sclerosis. She was healed of the MS and has been symptom-free for over three years now. She has been able to return to full-time nursing at a major hospital near her home in Colorado, enjoying an energetic busy life, and regularly gives copies of the book to others to encourage them!

One woman wrote that the practical principles she learned from the book have had a powerful healing impact on her marriage relationship!

Many have read the book twice, a few as many as four times, using it for meditation and as a study tool alongside their Bible. This has been my greatest hope…that it would stir people deeply to search God's Word to know Him better for themselves.

In November of 2011, I was approached by a gentleman who lives on the other side of the world. He asked my permission to translate the book into a language I had never dreamed of in my wildest imaginings! Within five short months that effort was realized. Funds to support this project were gifted by two people who believed it would greatly help others, allowing the distribution of 5,000 copies to be launched overseas in a region impacting seven nations! Clearly God is breathing life onto this book!

Many have asked for **His Word Healed Me** to be translated into **Spanish**. Thanks to Monica Bosque who created the preliminary translation. Thank you to Martha Sheppard who devoted months of translation effort to finalize the Spanish to be ready for publication. I am happy to report it will be released before summer of 2014.

A ministry team in Nigeria is interested in having the book produced over there, and a woman named Siah said after reading the book *three* times she knew she wanted to translate it to be available in Japanese! She has been working diligently on this project since August of 2013. Thank you Siah!

The AUDIO project was completed in October 2012 and launched via cdbaby, available for downloading through iTunes. Appreciation goes out to David Lopez for his faithful diligence and expertise in aiding me to make this dream a reality. Thank you to his sister Gina for planting the initial seed to help it begin to happen. Here is the link for the AUDIO:

http://www.cdbaby.com/cd/jacquelinpriestley

Once again Allyson Gideon has applied her creative genius to prepare **His Word Healed Me** to "go KINDLE" which happened in December of 2013.

I am grateful beyond words to all those who have come

alongside to help since the book's inception.

I am in awe of this extraordinary God who is generously breathing His heart into **His Word Healed Me** and taking care of each detail as it continues to blossom to reach lives. I continue to humbly pray that the Lord would see fit to use this book to touch and encourage people to have greater confidence in Him for their own lives.

May the blessing that rests on this book unfold uniquely in your life as you read!

Jacquelin Priestley

Acknowledgements

Heartfelt thanks to Sherry and Allyson, without whom this book would not have been published. They were literally "raised up" to push me through to the final completion of this project. They sacrificed hours of their time, researching the technical details to make it happen. Allyson diligently worked on the cover design and creation of the website, while Sherry tirelessly formatted the manuscript. The support of these two women as they "caught the vision" means more to me than I will ever be able to say.

Thanks to Judy, surgery scheduler in the doctor's office, for her time spent sharing "behind the scenes" insights about my case, and for her assistance in getting letters of permission from the doctors to be mentioned in my story. Her encouragement and support were an inspiration to me.

I would like to express my appreciation to Drs. Lowe, Baghdassarian, and Shanberg, – heroes all in their own right, committed to their passion: medicine. Who could count, I wonder, how many lives they have each impacted for good? Many thanks for their supportive responses when I told them about the book, and their willingness to let me mention the significant parts they played as I walked out my cancer-scare journey.

Thank you to the women of the PRT group – Allyson, Sherry, Susy, Treseen, Shari, and Lydia – who met together for several hours to review and critique the book, and pray over it and for the people whose lives I hope to bless...

Thank you to Julie who took her red pen in hand and screened every line for punctuation. An arduous task indeed! Your loving enthusiasm is so appreciated!

Many thanks to friends and family for holding me accountable with the pressing question, "How are you doing on the book?" Avah was the first to read the first fifty pages. Her helpful suggestions inspired me to continue to devote time and prayer in writing what was in my heart to share with others. My daughter Erica, and son David have also been very encouraging. Thanks you two for praying for me, knowing the many extra challenges that were in my life which could have deterred me from completing this project. Your love and prayers have meant so much.

Thank you to my mother, who touched my heart with words of great encouragement. She insisted that I keep writing no matter what, and believed I had something to share that would encourage many.

* * *

In loving memory of my Daddy,
Robert L. Schenck
I miss you, but I will see you again

CONTENTS

CONTENTS

Introduction

*"O Lord my God, I cried to You and
You have healed me!"*
Psalm 30: 2

When I heard "cancer" from my specialist, it gave
me cause to feel like my world might be unraveling, to
feel quite vulnerable, and to face my own mortality. I
turned to the Source I had relied on: God my Rock, and
His very practical Word on healing. I have consistently
been told I should write about this experience. Some
have gone so far as to say they thought God wanted to
use me to help and encourage others if they get tough
medical news. I began to have a sense of responsibility
about it; hence you are holding this book in your hands.

I hope to lift the heart of each one of you who shares
these pages with me as I tell what I did when confronted
with a report of cancer. Along with my story, I'm
providing a comprehensive look at the healing Scriptures
I meditated on continually, and the insights that led to
my knowing how to hold on to God in a crisis.

As Eleanor Roosevelt once said, "Women are like teabags; you never know how strong they are until they're put in hot water!" I can candidly say the journey I was launched upon was not one I ever would have volunteered for, but it had great value because it showed me that I really do believe what I thought I did, and more importantly, God is as real today as He shows Himself to be in the Bible. When a big challenge in life tested me, I once again found His promises carried me with remarkable results!

My hope and prayer is that this book will assist you in being securely anchored in the Scriptures and God's goodness concerning healing, and that any previously held doubts will melt away as truth is revealed to you and you are set free from unbelief. My prayer is that you will be encouraged and strengthened to say, *"As for me, I will choose to cling to the Word of God every time"* when it comes to healing.

I trust that this new confidence in His goodness and availability will also create a wonderful ripple effect which impacts all other areas of your life as well.

CHAPTER 1

Diagnosis

"...When the enemy shall come in like a flood, the
Spirit of the Lord will lift up a standard against him..."
Isaiah 59:19 (AMP)

The phone rang while I was studying in the living room. I answered, and a familiar voice greeted me and asked me if I was sitting down. When I said I wasn't, the caller suggested that I probably should. I couldn't believe my ears as I listened – I was being told by my long-time physician, Dr. Lowe, that he wasn't happy with the x-rays I had brought him the day before.

He told me he was going to refer me to a specialist immediately.

"We'll set you up for next week," he said. "No, actually, I'll have the staff call to see if they can make room for you to get in to see him today or tomorrow. This is urgent!

"We'll set you up for next week," he said. "No, actually, I'll have the staff call to see if they can make room for you to get in to see him today or tomorrow. This is urgent!

What he said next made me understand why he had wanted me sitting down...

Let me first retrace the events which preceded that phone call. For many weeks I'd been having an ever-increasing dull ache in my lower right back, too low, I thought, for the kidney area. It went from a sporadic ache to hurting all the time; the sense of throbbing and pressure caused me to not be able to feel completely relaxed or comfortable. I'd had kidney stones several times before in my right kidney, and wondered if that might be it. I had been hospitalized in my early twenties for a week with a severe infection in the right kidney, so I guessed I might be heading for a repeat experience. I stepped up my intake of water, and also added cranberry juice, hoping that would help. The water wasn't working as I had hoped. Within another week I was waking up at night with deep sharp twitches in my right lower back. At 2:30 a.m., I woke trembling with pain. I told my husband he needed to take me to the hospital right away. He suggested taking ibuprofen or perhaps going to a clinic. I am so glad I didn't!

It was the wee hours of Saturday, February 23, 2003, as I gratefully got into a hospital bed and received medication to help deal with the pain. X-rays verified I was passing several large kidney stones from the right kidney. It was during the taking of the x-rays that something was spotted on the *left* kidney, which hadn't been hurting me at all. Suddenly the insistent pain from the kidney stones on the right side had become my friend! Without it, I never would have known what had been quietly growing in my other kidney.

During the nine hours I remained in emergency, I was in and out of groggy sleep due to medication which brought blessed relief from the pain, but I remember quite a hubbub occurring at my bedside. The attending doctor said a second, more detailed x-ray would be needed. They asked if I had allergies to iodine. I didn't know and felt scared because years before I'd had a terrifying allergic reaction to penicillin that nearly killed me. The remote possibility of having another medical allergic reaction made me feel alarmed. I called my mother to check if she knew from my childhood if I had any allergies to iodine. When she said she could not recall but didn't think so, I didn't feel as reassured as I had hoped to! I asked her to pray for me, hung up, signed the form, and was wheeled into a room with some sort of specialized scanning machine, which I later learned was a CT scan.

As they began injecting the iodine dye into my arm, I closed my eyes and softly quoted, "When I am afraid, I will trust in Thee", (Psalm 56:3, KJV) because yes, I felt scared. I was in emergency, my right side was hurting like blazes from the kidney stones, and because of the weird, hushed way the doctors were acting and doing other tests so quickly, things had a very uncertain feeling. I made myself focus on that calming verse while

3

the nurses started the test. I also fought fear as I wondered if I would have a violent reaction to the iodine, still recalling the horror-filled experience of the allergic reaction to the penicillin. Within moments after they started the injection, I realized I was going to be okay with the iodine. What a relief! The scan produced a very clear picture of my left kidney with "something suspicious" on it. I was feeling no pain in the *left* kidney, but the test confirmed the presence of a mass they initially thought they had seen while testing the right one (which *had* been causing me pain).

The wee hours of Saturday in the ER had rolled over into Sunday morning. As I was released that morning, the attending doctor made me promise to contact my regular doctor immediately. I could not get him to tell me anything further, but promised I would follow up. The bigness of his eyes and the sound in his voice made me aware that what they had seen during the scan probably was not too good. Leaving the emergency room, I had a surreal sense of not being connected to the ground as I walked slowly back to the car. I was still hurting because of the right kidney. I wanted to cry. I felt like fear was hovering all around me, waiting for me to succumb to it, but I knew better. I decided to not allow myself to give voice to what the fear was whispering to me. I told the "What ifs" in my head to "Shut up!" Once home, I crawled into bed to sleep off the pain medications and escape from the residual pain. I also wanted to run away for a while from the scary feeling I had been left with while in the emergency ward.

The next day, I went back to the hospital early in the

morning to get my own copy of the x-rays. I signed for them and drove over to drop them off at Dr. Lowe's office. He said he would get to the x-rays later that morning, or by the following day, promising to call me as soon as he did. I had known him for 19 years and trusted him implicitly, so I said, "Okay," and felt peaceful and hopeful.

The next day was Tuesday and it would be a day I will never forget. I finished my half-day of work in the morning, and drove home with a foreboding feeling hanging over me about the recent weekend's events. I had mentally mapped out the remainder of my day, planning to get housework done for a couple hours, and then set aside time to study my Bible. As I started my planned housework, an insistent nudge in my gut kept pushing at me to set aside the housework, get out into the living room *first,* and get into the Scriptures immediately. "I will, I will," I answered back in my heart as I started the housework. Within ten minutes the nudge was so strong I stopped fighting it and took myself into the living room, Bible in hand. I knew that strong "nudge" was God telling me to read now. I grabbed my Bible and sat down on the sofa, situating myself with a cup of tea and notebook in hand.

The pages fell open to the Psalms and my eye fell on Psalm 30. The first four verses startled me because it suddenly felt very personal. **It was about being healed, and being rescued from death.**

In light of the circumstances that had transpired in the previous 48 hours, I definitely took note! Reading out loud, I meditated on Psalm 30, breathing the words in like a prayer. I usually study the Amplified Version of the Bible, and Psalm 30:1-4 said: "I will extol You, O Lord, for You have lifted me up and have not let my foes rejoice over me; O Lord my God, I cried to You and You have healed me. O Lord, You have brought my life up from Sheol (the place of the dead); You have kept me alive, that I should not go down to the pit (the grave). Sing to the Lord, O you saints of His, and give thanks at the remembrance of His Holy Name." Those words shook me, because I couldn't help wondering if I might be in for some pretty serious stuff.

I sat there thinking about what I was reading, as well as the irony and significance of my Bible "just happening" to fall open to those verses. As I read, I especially noticed the *tenses* of some of the words.

Before that dreaded phone call, I had been carefully reading verses two and three in particular, rather than just skimming them. The tense of the verb was as if it was already accomplished "You *have* healed me", not "*will* heal me." When I read verse three it really got to me: **"You kept me alive, that I should not go down to the pit (the grave)."**

I took verse three and meditatively broke it open like a piece of bread to chew on. There was a lot being said in that verse --

It was telling me:
    God would be my source.
    He would keep me in His care, and
    He would keep me alive (as opposed to me dying), and
    that I wouldn't go to the grave.

That was like music to my ears. Then I did what I

always do when I read my Bible - I personally received it as talking *to me*.

I conversationally prayed about what I was reading and said, "Okay God, I don't know what I'm in for, but I will immerse myself into every healing verse I can find! Help me to discover every possible insight as You did just now. I don't want to have any disease, Lord. I don't want a tumor growing in my body. I am trusting You to keep me alive and to heal me, just like it says in these verses." ...and that's when the phone rang...

...and that's when the phone rang...

I jumped up to answer the phone, leaving my open Bible on the couch in the living room. I was pleased to hear Dr. Lowe's voice. I've known him so long; he is a dear person, besides being my personal physician. He got straight to the point in telling me why he had called.

"Hi, Jackie dear, are you sitting down?" (He talks to me like I'm family).

"No Frank, should I be?" I answered. (My heart started to pound nervously.)

"Yes, I think so," he said. "Jackie, the x-rays don't look good." (Suddenly I started to feel out-of-body and slightly queasy. The room seemed to get grey, as if color left and everything turned into black and white and slow motion).

"They don't?" I answered. "What do you mean, Frank?"

"I don't like the look of the mass any more than the doctor in the ER did," he said. "We need to get you to a specialist right away," he explained.

"So, sometime next week, Frank?" I asked.

"No, that's not soon enough," he said. "It needs to happen right away – this is urgent."

I felt myself shrink on the inside when he said that. He proceeded to tell me about a colleague of his who specialized in kidney diseases, reassuring me I would be in good hands. When I asked him what he thought was going on in my body he answered, "You need to be prepared to lose your kidney."

As I listened in disbelief, the first thing that blurted out of me was a protest. "Nah aah. Nah aah!" (in the tone of a six year old who isn't getting her way). Having somebody tell you that you need to be prepared to lose your kidney is not exactly normal conversational fare!

"You need to be prepared to lose your kidney."

A Remarkable Experience

Simultaneously while having the conversation with Dr. Lowe, I had an experience that I will remember forever. It was one of the most unique spiritual experiences I have ever had yet. It carried me and gave me courage through all the scary moments in the three months that followed.

From the moment Dr. Lowe had said, "You need to be

sitting down," I started to have a deep, sick feeling of dread. When I heard him say, "You need to be prepared to lose your kidney," a gripping fear crept over me. It felt like it came from the floor up into my feet, rapidly creeping up my legs, like a quickly-growing sucking vine from a horror movie. I felt paralyzed while I listened to my heart pounding as if it would explode from fear. The dreadful feeling continued up my thighs and was just about at my mid-section, ready to grab at my heart with claw-like fingers, when I sensed a gentle but very strong love come over me. It was as if somebody was putting a cozy heated blanket on me, all around my head, my shoulders, and even reaching into my heart to protect me.

All the while, I could hear Dr. Lowe talking to me on the phone in my right ear, of course, but just as clearly on the inside of my *heart* were the strong words, "WHOSE REPORT WILL YOU BELIEVE?"

I knew immediately that was a thought right out of Isaiah 53:1. Then, gently but firmly came the words: "What did *I* just say to you out in the living room? What did *I* tell you? What were MY words to you in Psalm 30? Keep your eyes and your heart focused on MY report to you, on what MY Word says, despite what you are hearing right now. You keep your focus on ME!"

Those words were coming so powerfully to me in my heart they began to dominate the moment. Despite what Dr. Lowe's voice was telling me in my ear through the phone, just as real - internally and very distinctly - were these reassuring words coming to me like a loving force, vying for my attention. The words coming to my heart became even more insistent: "You listen to MY words,

9

child! You focus on what I just told you in My Word while you were reading in the living room!"

I later discovered a verse in Isaiah 59:19 that says, "When the enemy comes in like a flood, the Spirit of the Lord will raise up a standard against him." I thought that was quite amazing! The enemy was fear and a scary medical report. That *standard* was going to be God's Word, and I was going to discover that it would literally fight for me in the months ahead!

What was happening in that moment was a fulfilling of Scripture. God's love was fighting for me, protecting my heart and mind with a reminder of promises of healing. While circumstances and information from a medical report were trying to get me to receive fear, the promises I had studied rose up in my heart and became God-breathed and alive, with something to say to me as well! (II Timothy 3:15, 16, AMP).

God's loving presence was immediately there for me on a very practical level to raise up a standard *against fear* with His Word, which offered a far better report and a higher standard of hope and power from which to draw. *It was a living, loving shield for me.* As a protective parent would do for a frightened little child, it was as if I was having my chin tilted upward so I would look into "Daddy's eyes," into the eyes of my loving Heavenly Father. My faith was being powerfully stirred. I will never forget that amazing moment. The Prince of Peace had shown up to soothe and protect me while I was hearing scary medical speculation. In some of the gospels, when Jesus would teach the masses of people about God, He presented God as a tender and loving Heavenly Father. He spoke of God as "Abba Father" when He prayed. Abba literally translates as "Daddy."

As I experienced God's encouraging words in my heart during that phone call from my doctor, I felt a reversing of that sick, queasy fear that had begun to grip me. It literally retreated and was pushed right back down out of me, down my legs, back out my feet into the floor. The warm protected feeling continued to get stronger and became the dominant sense, causing me to feel safe. Dr. Lowe finished the call by telling me he would have the scheduler from the specialist's office call me with an appointment as soon as possible.

A Lifeline of Hope

Quite honestly, I do not know how long I sat there after that phone call. I decided that the Scriptures would be my lifeline of hope. I walked back into the living room, feeling a bit like a noodle. I sat down where I had left my Bible, knowing I needed to do some serious praying!

I was understandably rattled, yet paradoxically I was experiencing a sense of God's peace and presence. It occurred to me I had been reading the Scriptures in an extremely timely manner just prior to that phone call. The verses I had been reading on the pages that "just happened" to fall open were powerfully unique to my need.

I knew I wanted to draw as close to God as possible at that moment. I whispered a lot of dazed, "Thank You's" for those first four verses in Psalm 30.

I gave a "Thank You" for all the strong nudges I'd had

to reprioritize and get into the living room to read *first*, rather than do housework right away as I had planned. The timing had put a shield of protection and promise around me just prior to the call.

Only God could have known how much I was going to need to read those verses and have a quiet meditative time before getting that phone call! Having just spent time in those verses was the bridge used to talk to my heart and fight for me when fear was trying to get a death-grip on me. I opened my mouth and poured my heart out with gratitude in prayer:

"Thank You that You reminded me to think on Your Word while I was being told I would have to prepare to be cut open and have my kidney taken out!

"Thank You that Scripture tells me You will never leave me nor forsake me (Hebrews 13:5, AMP) and that You are the Lord God Who is my Healer (Exodus 15:26, AMP).

"Thank You that I know Your Name, Jesus. Thank You that I won't have to go through this alone and You will keep my life from going to the grave just like it says in Psalm 30:3 (AMP).

"Thank You that Your Word tells me I was healed by the stripes of Jesus. That means long before I was ever born God, You knew I would be in this moment, with *this* news, and You had already prepared the answer to meet my need through the power of what You have accomplished in Jesus"... and on I prayed for quite a while. I didn't pray fear, I prayed God's word.

I gave thanks to God for His solutions. I prayed what

Scripture teaches, rather than praying helplessness or dread of what the doctor had told me. I think many people would have naturally called their family members and friends right away, crying hard and talking cancer. They would have heard themselves telling others that they have cancer and were going to lose their kidney, and it would have snowballed from conversation to conversation.

I didn't pray fear, I prayed God's Word.

I decided *not* to call my parents, daughter, son, or any friends for the moment. I decided to hunker down into God's Word and be very still in order to stay in that peaceful safe place I was experiencing. My mind and heart were still, yet actively focusing on the Scriptures that held promises of overcoming - promises of life, of healing, and hope. I did not want to shatter that peace with chatty phone conversations about the doctor's report. I also did not want to be pressed to explain the details of anything because I knew someone would voice that "c" word I didn't want to say or hear...

The Kidney Has to Be Removed

GROWTH. MASS. TUMOR. CANCER. The words nobody ever wants to hear. It wasn't until I was sitting in the office of the specialist recommended to me by Dr. Lowe, that I realized he had never spoken the word "cancer" to me during that initial phone call. God bless him for that! I truly came to appreciate that he had not said the "c" word, as I began to call it, because it helped me keep fear at bay, leaving more room for getting aggressive with my faith. I determined that would be my policy for myself - I thought about what I was dealing with, and if and when I would talk to anyone else about it. I knew the words I let run through my mind, as well as out of my own mouth, would be key in whether I stayed built up in faith and focused on God, or whether I let fear in. Fear and cancer are like cousins that run hand-in-hand, and I didn't want either one of them gaining any ground in me.

A day-and-a-half after that phone call I found myself sitting in the waiting room of the doctor that was highly recommended by Dr. Lowe. He specialized in kidney diseases and cancers. His name was Dr. Baghdassarian.

Dr. Lowe said he had known him for years and he was one of his most trusted colleagues, so I felt quite secure about going to see him. He was a surgeon as well (that part made me nervous because I was hoping to *not* need surgery. I wanted this whole "lose your kidney" thing to just go away!), and I was assured by Dr. Lowe that he was one of the best in the area.

Fear and cancer are like cousins that run hand-in-hand, and I didn't want either one of them gaining any ground in me.

That's Not Acceptable!

The news I got from the kidney specialist was very

discouraging. After a quick introduction and brief explanation as to why I was there, the doctor studied the package of x-rays I had brought from the scans taken at the emergency ward.

He turned, looked at me, and said point blank, "Oh yes, we'll definitely have to remove the kidney."

Everything from that moment on felt like slow motion. When I asked, "Why!?!" he told me he saw tumors all the time, this was fairly large, and the safest thing for us to do for my well-being was to remove the kidney. I asked what did the surgery entail, and what kind of cut was involved. (To date I didn't have a mark on me, not a scar or stretch mark. I did not like the idea of being cut open or scarred!)

Dr. Baghdassarian proceeded to explain the cut would go from the general left part of my mid-section near the belly-button all the way around my side to the back near the kidney. My brain started fogging over as I heard what he was telling me. The only thing that I could think of inside my head was, *That's not acceptable!*"

Needless to say, I had no desire to be sliced open like a big watermelon! To my surprise, without even thinking about it, the words, "THAT'S NOT ACCEPTABLE!" blurted out my mouth.

He looked startled for a split second and then he continued on with his explanation. He told me the mass appeared to be contained and centrally located in the kidney area. He said he would schedule a series of thorough tests on me which would reveal whether anything had metastasized anywhere else in my body; once those tests verified what he was hoping for, we would set a date for my surgery.

He shook my hand warmly, smiled, and walked out of the office. I sat there alone, with the echo of his words all around me.

I DIDN'T CRY – I WAS NUMB. Cut me open? Remove my kidney? Spread anywhere else in my body? I felt like I was living through a bad dream. When I stood to put my x-rays back in the big envelope, I felt like I was pushing through thick Jell-O, every move took effort. I could hardly get my fingers to be coordinated enough to handle the x-rays and get them back into the folder. Then I walked down the hallway on legs that felt like overcooked spaghetti noodles.

I kept thinking, "That's not acceptable. That is just *not* acceptable."

I came to the conclusion weeks later that the strong internal response of, **"That's Not Acceptable"** was most likely the voice of my faith keeping guard over my own heart. It was not denial; it was my faith talking - not allowing fear in, not letting doubt in, and not just rolling over and letting me accept what I was hearing. I think too many people do that when they get scary medical news. *Instead of looking to God, they are in shock and just accept what they are being told*, as if what the doctor is saying is their only possibility.

Calls with bad news become like a declaration of doom. It begins to gain momentum like a snowball trying to become an avalanche.

Additionally, they make what I respectfully consider to be a mistake by telling everyone they know the scary diagnosis, so it is repeated and repeated out of their own mouth. Everybody begins to "agree that it's so," even though they hope it isn't. Bad news can become like a declaration of doom. It begins to gain momentum like a snowball trying to become an avalanche.

I wanted nothing to do with that whole scenario. I called Dr. Lowe later that same afternoon and told him I didn't like the specialist he had sent me to! Dr. Lowe immediately pegged it - it was not actually that I didn't like Dr. Baghdassarian; it was that I did not like what he was *telling* me.

I told Dr. Lowe I was frustrated because I had become mentally numb during the appointment and had forgotten to ask the specialist the questions I had meant to ask. I told him I felt angry (I am told that is a common response) because it did not seem right that someone could walk into a room, barely say hello, announce one of your organs needed to be yanked out (which, of course, is *not at all* how the doctor had put it!), shake your hand, and then walk back out of the room!

Dr. Lowe patiently listened to me whine. He assured me he would speak with Dr. Baghdassarian on my behalf so I could go see him again. Within a couple days I was back in the specialist's office.

"Well, young lady," he said with a twinkle in his eye, "I see you're back! Dr. Lowe told me you weren't happy with our first meeting. He let me know you are a long-time patient and friend of his. I can assure you I will take all the time you need to get your questions answered, and I will be sure you get the very best of care."

We got out the x-rays again and he showed me how to understand what was appearing on the film. I still felt a weird, far away, foggy sense the whole time we were talking (I later realized that was all part of mental shock as I was attempting to process what I was hearing and seeing on the x-rays), but I felt a lot better because he was so kind and patient with me.

A No-Win Situation

The old cliché "I'm between a rock and a hard place" came to mind. As the doctor and I talked, I asked if we could go in surgically and not assume the tumor was something that would cause me to lose my kidney. (I never called the tumor the "c" word).

"Couldn't we just remove the mass and leave the rest of the kidney alone?" I asked. "Maybe it would be benign". (*Benign* means no cancer; *malignant* means cancer).

That is when he broke it down so I could understand what we were seeing on the x-ray and what I was up against. The x-ray showed the tumor was located *centrally* in the area where the urine is created in the kidney. The kidney acts as a filter. Waste is produced and gathered into that central area, changed into urine, and then released through tubes (called ureters) that lead to the bladder. From there we release it from our bodies.

The doctor explained that the centralized location of the tumor in the kidney was a key factor. Even if they got in there and found it was benign, it was sizeable –

which meant it was *growing* - and cutting the tumor out would render the kidney useless.

What frustration! It seemed clear the kidney would be lost either way. *I was apparently faced with a no-win situation.* Since he had taken the time to help me understand what I was looking at on the x-ray, I could clearly see what he was talking about. *As much as I didn't like it, these were the medical facts, staring me in the face.*

Years ago I had studied to be an Emergency Medical Technician (EMT). I had learned enough to know that there was no way around what the doctor was showing me and telling me - no way around it naturally speaking, that is.

It would have been very easy (and natural) to feel stuck at that point, and just say to myself, "Well, I guess I'm going to have to lose my kidney."

After all, the doctor from the emergency room, then my own doctor, and now a kidney specialist/surgeon had all let me know it was not good. And now I could also see for myself from the x-ray *the mass was in the worst spot in the kidney.*

But the reactive phrase, "That's not acceptable!" kept rising up on the inside of me like a broken record! That thought wouldn't let go of me. I asked Dr. "B" if he could recommend another doctor. I told him I did not want to work with anyone else, because Dr. Lowe had recommended him so emphatically, but I would feel more responsible to myself if I got another opinion because of the seriousness of it. He recommended a doctor across town.

Meanwhile, Dr. "B" said he wanted to set me up for a series of tests to check my blood, bone marrow, intestinal area, and my other organs. He wanted to verify nothing had metastasized. *Metastasized* is a polite word for a very rude concept. It means cancer has spread and anchored itself in other locations and organs, or perhaps spread throughout the entire body, which is obviously deadly.

It was a long walk from the doctor's office back to my car. It was a beautiful sunny California day, but was no longer a typical day for me. "Typical" had completely disappeared a week ago, when I first got the news about the mass growing in my left kidney. Each step echoed the word "metastasized". It all felt weird and other-worldly, like a strange bad dream - one I did not want to be starring in, that was for sure!

I was nervous about the impending tests. I knew I had choices about what to focus on – I figured I had two major "c" words in my life: the bad "c" word, which I never once allowed myself to speak, and the Life "C" word - <u>C</u>hrist, the Son of the Living God, my Redeemer, Savior and HEALER, who I would turn to as my Rock and personal physician.

I did not know yet if perhaps looming in the future was another "c" word: chemotherapy. I did not know the details that would be played out in the journey I was on. I decided I had better fight hard to not allow my "Panavision and Technicolor" imagination to take me internally to all the "what ifs" of things going badly.

I refused to allow my mind to envision going through chemo. Not once. *Not once.* I didn't permit mental drama or worry scenarios. I did not let myself research or learn about chemo. So far, I spoke of all these things I was dealing with to no one but God. I felt like I had been pushed over a cliff edge, and He was my lifeline!

I kept my mind on the Word of God, because it was my source and supply, my resting place, and my hope. It was what gave me courage, and was my provision. There is a verse that states, "Thou wilt keep him in perfect peace whose mind is stayed (or fixed) on Thee" (Isaiah 26:3, KJV). I was determined to keep my thoughts in that place of peace. *I treated God's Word as if it were an open intravenous line for courage straight into my heart and thoughts.* Every doctor's appointment and what they said were opportunities to be afraid, but instead I would choose to remind myself out loud of what God said and what He had ALREADY done for me in all the healing verses.

I saw God's Word literally as medicine

Instead of anticipating chemo-therapy, I was busy filling my mind and heart with God's promises as my "treatments". Not two times a week, not once a day, but every free moment. I listened to teaching tapes in the car about healing. I made tapes for myself reading the healing verses so I could hear them over and over. I made large, brightly-colored poster signs with healing verses on them, and taped them on the walls in my house. I made 3-by-5 cards with healing verses on them to meditate on word by word, and remind me to give thanks for God's promises. I could not shoot His Word into my vein like an intravenous (I.V.) treatment, but I could put God's healing word like a medicine into my understanding.

The more I filled up on His Word, the more my soul prospered. I believed my body would catch on as well, and be blessed all the way down to the cellular level. There would be one dominant "C" word in my life – Christ Jesus - and not that horrid other "c" word: cancer. This was III John 2 in action. It reads, "Beloved, I pray that you may prosper in all things and be in health, just as your soul prospers." *My soul was prospering by feeding on God's Word*, and I trusted it was producing health and healing in my flesh, just like it says it will in Proverbs 4:20-22 (AMP).

Throughout the whole experience, I never struggled with or thought a "Woe is me" or a "*Why me* God?" type of feeling... not for a moment. So often we *do* hear people ask the "Why me?" question, wondering "Why is *God* letting this happen *to me*?" That is certainly a reasonable question coming from a human heart that feels overwhelmed!

I think sometimes hidden in the middle of those types of questions people are really struggling more with a sense of almost *blaming* God, because they are feeling hurt, angry, and scared, but blaming won't help our hearts to be open to *trust* or *receive the help we need*. For myself, I also knew self-pity would not serve me well either, so I needed to avoid it if I could.

I was dealing with serious stuff. I knew I might even be in for the fight of my life, but I did not blame God. How could I? He was kind to give me a "heads up" by permitting me to have the kidney stones (an experience that can be painful, but is not dangerous). That, in turn, had served in getting me to the emergency room because of the pain, and it was there that I found out about the mass on the left kidney, which actually *was* serious.

He didn't have to do that! I saw His grace watching out for me. I also knew that everything in His Word tells me He is good, that He loves me, that He is my Provider and Healer, Redeemer and Friend, so I knew He would be God for me as I turned to Him. The Lord has a consistent track record throughout Scripture, especially demonstrated in the person of Jesus Christ, His Son. It all showed me that He is generous beyond measure. Any person with an excellent reputation or character can be trusted. How much more, therefore, could I trust God Who is always faithful? It was logical.

Quick Scripture References - Chapter One

Psalm 56:3 ...when afraid, will trust in Thee KJV
Psalm 30:1-4 I cried to You, You have healed me AMP
Isaiah 53:1 Who will believe the report of the Lord? NKJV
Isaiah 59:19 Spirit raised up a standard...NKJV
II Timothy 3:15, 16 Every Scripture is God-breathed AMP
Hebrews 13:5 God will never leave or forsake us AMP
Exodus 15:26 God is the Lord Who heals me AMP
Psalm 30:3 ...You have kept me alive... AMP
Isaiah 26:3 ...perfect peace...fix mind on God...KJV
III John 2 ...prosper, be in health as your soul prospers NKJV
Proverbs 4: 20-22 ...His Word is health and healing AMP

*   *   *

CHAPTER 2

My Battle Plan

*"Do not let this Book of the Law depart from your
mouth; meditate on it day and night...
Be strong and courageous..."*
Joshua 1:8, 9 (AMP)

SEVEN DAYS HAD PASSED since first going to
emergency, and Sunday was finally here. I was still
hurting somewhat in the right kidney as the last of the
smaller stones passed, but wanted to get myself to
church. I didn't have the energy to go to my own church,
a distance from home, so I went to one close to my
house where I also knew the pastor. I wanted to see him
and do what is instructed in the Bible in James 5:14
when sickness or disease hits. I wanted to be prayed for,
be anointed with oil, and ask God for healing. I knew I
needed God.

Not only was I facing a major surgery, but it was clear
I might be facing something even scarier. While sitting

in church, something came to mind I had said earlier in the month that was really ugly. It jarred me, and also concurrently reminded me there was a part in James 5 that I had forgotten about. *An important part for receiving healing is explained in James 5:16* (NIV). It talks about confessing our sins to one another so that we might be healed. I was being reminded of that awful moment so I could make it right, because it's a clean heart that can receive blessing. My heart was being corrected for my own good as this Scripture was being brought to my remembrance.

The ugly thoughts had occurred because for several months prior to the kidney diagnosis there had been a lot of strife in my home. Every little thing turned into an argument and I was deeply discouraged about several significant issues that couldn't seem to get resolved. It had really been getting to me and I had become quite depressed. After my husband had walked out of the room from yet another fight between us, I had thought to myself in my heart first, and then actually *said* out loud to myself:

> "You need to die Jackie. You are just a stupid person and you can't get relationships right. You just need to die. You need to be dead. You aren't worth anything to anybody. Yep, you need to die; you're just a loser."

That is some pretty extreme and horrid stuff to *think*, let alone permit to come out of your own mouth! I must admit, at the time when I said that, it even startled *me* and I thought, "Woe, that's pretty intense!", but then I shook it off and went about my business doing the dishes in the kitchen.

During that first week after getting the "lose-your-kidney" news, I recalled the verse in the book of James that warns, "Where there is strife, there is every evil work." I was daily pursuing Scripture to receive healing from God, but it was as if evil was trying to undermine me in every way possible through strife.

Fear had not been able to penetrate my mind or heart, but my home had steadily turned into a hornet's nest. To have *thought* such ugliness and then yielded to it by also *saying* something like that over myself, I had made myself vulnerable to "every evil work". It had the trademark of darkness all over it! From God's loving perspective, those thoughts and words were full of death and destruction.

Now I was in church to get real with God, ask for prayer, and ask Him to touch me with healing. In a flash of understanding I knew what I had to do. I had to do the tattle-on-myself "confess your sins" part in James 5:16 (NIV). I cringed with the thought of it, but I didn't argue inside. I knew I had to be humble.

After the service I approached the pastor and said, "I might have a serious medical issue on my hands," and asked if he and the elders would lay hands on my head in prayer, and anoint me with oil. He was immediately agreeable and said he would get some people together. I went into a separate area to wait while he got the elders and brought them to pray for me.

Once they all gathered, right in front of the pastor, the elders, and my husband (who had no idea what I was about to say, and boy, was he stunned!), I told them that before they prayed for me I needed to repent about

27

something in order to come in line with James 5:16 (NIV). I explained what had transpired in my thoughts and come out of my mouth a month earlier - that I had said I was a loser and should be dead.

I looked at all of them and said, "I need to repent to the Lord for my ugly-heartedness, for my foolish and sinful words, and for allowing my own mouth to speak such disrespectful and dishonoring words over myself. I confess before you guys and God that my attitude and words were evil in God's sight."

I continued, "Jesus warns about life and death being in the power of the tongue. I bring those words to the foot of the cross and put myself under the protective power of the blood of Jesus. I got convicted about this during the service. I don't want to put a breach in God's protective hedge of grace around me, or let the devil take potshots at my life by giving him permission to do so with such foolish words!"

They were all looking at me rather astonished, but I didn't care. I did not say all that to impress *them* (on the contrary, my own ego and level of embarrassment would have loved to not "tattle" on myself!) or sound religious. I did it to put myself before a holy God so James 5:14, 15, and 16 could be fulfilled in my life to meet my need for healing. I knew that each doctor I had dealt with thus far believed the mass on my left kidney was cancer. *This was no time to be playing games or operating in half-truths while trying to receive fulfilled promises from the Word of God!* What I was dealing with was very real, so I needed to be very real with God even though it made me embarrassed!

When we prayed together I quoted healing verses over myself, and asked for very specific things:

- I asked for God to heal me completely

- I asked for God to protect me to not have that "c" word, and if it *was* that, to change it

- I asked Him to not let it spread anywhere else in my body

- I asked to not have to lose my left kidney

- I asked to be able to leave the hospital after the surgery with two healthy, fully-functioning kidneys

- I also asked God to cause me to heal after the surgery without any complications and no bad scars

Even as I explained what the doctors' reports were, I used the expression "the bad 'c' word" while talking with Pastor and the elders. Even when I prayed I used that phrase also and told God that I knew that *He knew* what I meant. I kept that discipline over my own words throughout the whole process of believing for my healing. I refused to tolerate saying that word.

The Word makes it clear God heals and restores people. He does not will them to lose body parts and organs!

The others prayed for God's mercy, then one of them prayed, "If it be Thy will for her to lose her kidney..." which I was very uncomfortable with, but I understood he was trying to "cover all the bases" when he prayed. That was clearly *not* prayer based on Scripture. The Word makes it clear God heals and restores people. He does not will them to lose body parts and organs!

I realized many people who love God are not necessarily trained or well-practiced in the power of literally praying the Word of God over people's needs.

Anyway, all I knew was I had held myself accountable to be obedient to what the Bible instructs us to do in James 5:14-16 when we are plagued with sickness, and I would be trusting God for results.

There were hugs all around. As I left, they all said they hoped to see me next week, and to be sure to let them know how I was doing. As I walked away I looked over my shoulder, flashed a grin, and said, "I'll be doing *great* because it is written 'the Lord is my God who heals me' and 'by the stripes of His Son I was healed'!" I was declaring *God's promise*, quoting His words out of Isaiah 53, and also Exodus 15:26, and trusting His Word to be backed by His faithfulness and His power.

Some might read my words of admitting a horrible attitude and say, "Gee whiz, Jackie, you're too hard on yourself. God understands when we get depressed and mouth off. It's not that big a deal." People might offer that to give me comfort, but those words are actually an accidental form of deception.

In the Old Testament, in fact throughout all of Scripture, it is clear that God takes words very seriously, and whenever people didn't take *His* words seriously, He was extremely displeased.

In the New Testament Jesus also taught we would literally be judged for every careless word we have spoken (Matthew 12:36, 37, NIV).

I have prayed about what Jesus meant when He warned about careless words, because His comment surprised and disturbed me. I realized God has a very different perspective than we do about the use of words. We are flip with words, but He isn't. It is clear when our thoughts are not renewed to what Scripture teaches, we are not Christ-conscious or Word-aware, the way He would like us to be. That doesn't mean we don't believe in God or love Him, not at all. It just means that our awareness of how He thinks and speaks is very underdeveloped on a practical level. That is why I had to hold myself accountable before God and His Word for that wretched stuff I had said about myself. I was trying to learn to be more aware of Him and how He wants me to think and speak.

My entire objective was to get myself right before God, to bring the polluted thinking in my heart to Him, admit it as vile from *His* perspective, and then also get forgiveness as it says in I John 1:9, "He is faithful and just to forgive us of our sins and to *cleanse us* from all unrighteousness." To have the words "It's not that big a deal," spoken to me as attempted comfort would not have been good for me to hear. If I had taken that stance instead of the one I did, I would have been doing what I John 1:8 warns about - I would have been saying I *hadn't* sinned by saying those ugly thoughts, and thereby put myself in a position of self-deception, according to that verse. Something like that could have been a detail that could have blocked me from receiving healing.

> *God's pattern all through the Word is this:*
> *He corrects so He can heal and restore.*

It definitely would have been more comfortable to *not* make it any kind of a big deal and gloss over what I had said, but deep inside I would have known I was wrong, and that I was not obeying God's nudge of correction. *He only corrects us to love us and heal us!* Not obeying would have created guilt. Guilt is unproductive! God's wisdom is in details. I see it all through His Word. Details concerning the condition of the heart matter to God. He corrected me so He could heal me. That is His pattern all through the Word: He corrects so He can heal and restore.

The Words I Chose to Speak

A week later I had another test, with yet more discouraging confirmations. I hated hearing that "c" word. When I received the news from the doctor, I got in the car and just sat there. How do you run errands after being told you have cancer and have to lose your left kidney? How do you see the road clearly to drive back to your house after news like that? Everything feels different.

After a moment, I put the key in the ignition. "Lord?" I said. Silence. No nudges, just quiet. What I noticed though was *this* time I did not feel afraid. Strange, out-of-body, stunned – Yes! I felt all those things, but I did not feel fearful or panicked. There was that "peace that passes understanding" thing happening for me again. It was pretty amazing. The verse came to mind again that says God will keep in peace the person who keeps his mind fixed on Him. (Isaiah 26:3, NLT).

I was beginning to understand that peace was not so much a place or a state of being as it was a *Person.* Those verses we hear at Christmastime about the prophecies of the infant King and His names... "Wonderful, Counselor, Mighty God, Everlasting Father, Prince of Peace, Emmanuel – God with us" (Isaiah 9:6 and Matthew 1:23) were all becoming even more of a reality on a very practical level, meeting me at every step of this journey.

I thought more and more about the importance of my words reflecting faith in God's Word. I continued with my decision to not tell my family for the time being. Even in the name of being on a prayer list to get prayer, I still didn't want people associating my name with that bad "c" word as I called it. I did not want a concert of voices saying and agreeing I had cancer as they called one another on the phone to pray for me!

I have some select friends who know how to hold on to the promises of God's Word when it comes to healing. They do it boldly, humbly, trusting and believing God's Word without hesitation. They were the only people I decided to call. Even talking with my spiritual confidants, I never once allowed myself to say that "c" word. I continued my discipline of faith, deciding to not rehearse the report of the doctors in my head, or talk about it; but rather to consistently repeat the report of God's Word (the healing promises) over myself and my body.

Focusing on Words of Life, Not Death

Weeks had passed since that 2:30 a.m. trip to the emergency ward on February 23. It was now mid-March. With all those tests and x-rays, I kept hoping somewhere I would get news that the mass had disappeared, or at least gotten smaller. Unfortunately each test confirmed the stance the doctors were taking – that I would have to lose my kidney. As for me, "That's not acceptable!" still kept ringing persistently on the inside of me! What the tests and doctors were saying didn't match what the Word said! I liked the report of the Lord much better!

With two-week gaps between appointments, I had to keep my mind protected and my faith strong. I figured God could certainly zap me with healing in an instant, but I was also aware that healing could be His *process* in my body. I approached God and His Word as my Source and my "treatment center". I didn't care which way I got it – either in an instant or as a process – e*ither way it would be God* and I was going after receiving healing!

RECEIVING HEALING has as much to do with what we *do* say, think, and believe, as with what we *don't* permit ourselves to say or think or believe. Scripture teaches us we had better not be double-minded when we seek God in prayer. It all works together. Before we go any further, notice the first two words in that sentence: *Receiving healing.* That implies someone needs to actively receive. I figured that someone was me. (God isn't the One that had a need!)

The issue is not talking God into doing something, but rather receiving what He clearly says in His Word He has *already done for us.* I disciplined myself to not say that I had the bad "c" word that all the medical people were saying I had. The reason I know this is all tied together (God's words, believing and trusting Him - and receiving) is because **Jesus explained in the gospels**, particularly in Matthew 12:34, **"Out of the abundance of the heart, the mouth speaks."** There was a definitive link there. I needed to have increased awareness about what was in my heart in abundance, and also what I gave permission to come out of my mouth. It was *imperative I didn't let my heart receive the report of cancer or start to let myself think or say,* "Well, I guess they're right. I guess I will have to lose my kidney," because it would have depleted my ability to rely on God and His power.

Believing, saying, and thinking all have to be aligned so there is no duplicity of thought as we approach God for help. In James 1:6, 7 (NIV) we're warned to *not* be double-minded, and Joshua 1:7-9 teaches that to have good success in obedience, we are not to let God's words depart from being in our mouths!

God teaches us in Deuteronomy 6:1-9 that we are to remember and speak His Word. We are to build our lives around His Word. It says we are to speak of Him and His words when we rise, when we lie down, when we walk, and when we go on our way (live our life).

He clearly wants us to be very diligent about being *saturated with His Word, and He wants us to know how He thinks.* Joshua 1:9 is especially amazing... it says God wants us to be that focused on His Word so He can bless us, causing us to have good success and deal wisely in our lives! It isn't to make us "religious"; it's for very practical blessing in daily life! God even uses the word "prosper" in those verses.

I KNEW GOD'S WORD would be a living shield of protection to me. **I knew His strength and power were impregnated within His Word,** and it would keep me close to Him and heal me. Another reason I wanted to practice Word-discipline was because of a promise I found in Hebrews 4:12, Amplified Version. It says God's Word is *alive*, so I knew it would be actively working within me around the clock:

"For the Word that God speaks is alive and full of power [making it active, operative, energizing, and effective]; it is sharper than any two-edged sword, penetrating to the dividing line of the breath of life (soul) and [the immortal] spirit, and of joints and marrow [of the deepest parts of our nature], exposing and sifting and analyzing and judging the very thoughts and purposes of the heart."

This gave me a visual of His words being a living and powerful "treatment" going into me, coursing through my system, and going after enemy cells that were out to get me. I also especially liked the "sharper than any two-edged sword" part, because I thought of it as being even more precise than a surgeon's knife.

Scripture says God is not only Love, but He is Light and Life. I could picture His Word going into me like a laser, removing cells that were a danger to me. It was exciting, because applying these principles of how His power works within us meant I had recourse for what I was being told medically, and for what the x-rays showed test after test. *I knew I was not limited to only what was available medically. I also had a powerful "report of healing" to cling to through God's Word.*

I could hold on to the power of *His* report while also trusting Him to bless to my advantage any help which medical science might offer. *ALL* the power to ultimately cause anything good to happen was *His*. If I filled my mind, heart, and mouth with *God*'s Word, then I could safely be assured my words would be speaking life as HE defines it. That is the arena of faith in which His power and goodness can show up, rather than one that speaks words full of doubt, fear, defeat, sickness, or helplessness.

Meanwhile, what My Heavenly Father said about disease, sickness, and healing in His Word was very clear, so I knew what His will was because *His Word and His will are the same.*

When fear tries to seize us in its grip, God's words and promises will rise up and fight for us if we have stored them in our hearts!

I have learned the wisest time to form the habit of consistently meditating on the healing verses is when we don't need them! I think of it as making sure my storehouse is full. At the very least, by forming that habit we will be building our faith and have a sense of God's loving provision as accessible and available. We may even become a source of encouragement to others. But if that personal tsunami ever hits, our storehouse will be full, ready for the storm, and we will know what to do and how to take a stand. When fear tries to seize us in its grip, God's words and promises will rise up and fight for us if we have stored them in our hearts!

That is what I experienced. I had always believed this in theory, because Scripture says in Isaiah that God raises up His standard to fight off the enemy – it was amazing to discover it really *did* happen, and that His standard (His Word) jumped into action when the scary report came knocking at *my* door. I knew because of God's Word I did not have to sign the "receipt book" and accept disease!

Answering in Faith When People Asked About Me

I was careful about who I talked with regarding the doctor's diagnosis. I protected myself with the arsenal of God's Word. I was in a war - a war I could not afford to lose.

People would express concern, asking what further results were coming from all the tests. The most frequently asked question was, "Well, what does the *doctor* say?" I would reply, "The doctor is of the opinion that the bad 'c' word is growing in my body, but I am clinging to a different 'C' Word, and that Word is Christ Jesus my Savior and Healer. I am clinging to God's report and promise that 'By His stripes ye were healed' and 'He sent His Word and He healed me'." (Isaiah 53:5 and Psalm 107:20)

I was keenly aware of how I answered because I wanted to honor the Lord as much as possible by keeping my words in line with His words. People told me that hearing me talk and answer that way greatly influenced the way they prayed for me. They said it helped them take a stand for healing with me and gave them something with which to agree. They said it reminded them to keep their focus on what the Scriptures said, the same way I was, rather than spending energy worrying over what the doctor's report was. Sure, it took guts for me to decide to answer that way, but I did not want any duplicity in my thinking or speech. I wanted to be as focused as a laser beam!

Friends said it helped them begin to grasp that I was not limited to what was going on in my body or limited to what the doctors said. They said it gave them courage to believe that maybe Christ really *was* bigger than a report of cancer. I wanted *those* kinds of prayers being prayed over me, rather than what I call "worry prayers," which though well-meant and full of care, can also be full of fear and doubt.

Not Denial, but Clinging to God

Scripture says God is Light and His Word is Light. According to Hebrews 4:12 (most thorough in the Amplified version) God's Word will be like a finely precisioned laser used in an intricate surgery!

We can trust His Word to work in us despite a doctor's report. I trusted God's Word during that three month period prior to the surgery – February 23 to May 3 -- even though the reports of oncologists, several specialists, and x-ray after x-ray all said "cancer" and "remove the kidney"! This did not mean I was being in denial. Rather, I was choosing where I was going to anchor my heart, my thoughts, and my confidence (faith), so that I could receive *His Word* personally to produce in my life, in my particular area of need.

"Mind over Matter" versus Reaching for God

For those reading this who might be of the mind-over-matter genre, I would *never* try to come up against cancer or any other disease with mere mind-over-matter, positive thinking, or positive "self talk" attempts. Cancer turns the cells of people's bodies against them! Wishful thinking may be that we can talk ourselves out of it, but the statistics certainly say otherwise. I knew I couldn't "will" this thing to go away. Rather, I was bringing my need to and trusting the power of a Person (God my Healer) to combat the diagnosis, hitting it hard with the authority of His Word.

Sometimes denial can be another part of mind-over-matter thinking. I did not play that game, attempting to trick myself by denying what was happening in my body and calling that "acting in faith" or being positive. Denial is just that: denial.

I **didn't** go around saying "I'm not sick, I don't have a tumor. I'm not sick, I don't have a tumor," like a parrot, trying to *will* myself or psyche myself into having enough positive thoughts that the medical facts would go away! That would have been nonsense.

I **didn't** try to convince myself the doctors were wrong or the x-rays were not real. I stood side-by-side with each oncologist and specialist, asking them to teach me to understand my own x-rays as we talked. The medical facts were *very* real.

I **didn't** rely on myself or my own will power or the power of positive thinking at all. That is *not* what I was doing. I knew Who my Source of Hope and Power was. I know that Jesus Christ is the "C" Word of the ages, and He was my Source. I figured He healed then, He would heal now, and He would heal *ME*!

When I was trusting Jesus for healing despite the specialists' reports, sometimes I would read the Scriptures very loudly. I didn't care if I felt silly or weird – I would holler and cry out in prayer to Jesus, "Son of David, have mercy on me!" because I wanted to do and copy what I saw in the Word of God. I wanted His compassion to move on my behalf and receive healing in my body.

I wanted my circumstances to be changed by Jesus, just like it was for those who were healed in the Bible. With childlike faith and boldness I copied what I saw *them* do, and those folks often hollered at Jesus on the top of their lungs, crying out to Him for mercy!

I figured He healed then, He would heal now, and He would heal ME!

Because my need was hidden in an internal organ where I could not see if something happened or not, I would give God thanks for being moved by compassion and for being true to Himself on my behalf, whether I felt anything or not. I would declare loudly that He was the same yesterday, today, and forever, and that He was my Healer (Hebrews 13:8, NIV).

I would holler according to Isaiah 53:1-5 that He fulfilled that prophecy and I was healed by His stripes, just as Scripture says. I would let God know I was one of the ones who *would* believe His report, since He was asking in the verses if anybody would. I decided I was one of the ones who would tenaciously believe!

I had to shout so that faith was louder inside me than the storm was.

Set Like Flint, Not Double-Minded

DURING MY QUEST FOR HEALING I was stretching myself to learn to do whatever I saw people do in the Word... Shouting praise, hollering the Word of God over myself, shouting the Name of Jesus as my source was not the norm for me! But I was in a storm of sorts and I needed to shout fear away: I had to shout so that *faith was louder inside me than the storm was.*

I can honestly say during the days and weeks that followed my initial diagnosis, the majority of the time a genuine peace stayed with me and even increased. It carried me on a daily, hour-by-hour basis, and only occasionally did I experience momentary panic or fear. The rest of the time I had tremendous peace. It was the result of being so focused on Christ and the abundance of healing verses. Now that I think about it, when the few people who knew the circumstances would make comments, "Oh, you're going through so much right now," I would almost feel removed from it. Obviously, I never would have volunteered for the journey I was on, but all the meditating on the Scriptures I was doing was having a wonderful side effect - it was causing me to be in God's Presence so much, I was predominantly full of peace and even joy. I was experiencing the tangible fulfilling of the two verses that say "...the joy of the Lord is your strength" (Nehemiah 8:10) and also "In His Presence is fullness of joy" (Psalm 16:11) as I lived out the journey I was on.

The surgery date had been set for May 3rd. As each week passed while I waited for that day to arrive, I continued aligning my heart and words with His Word, making sure I had no duplicity of thought or spirit. James 1:5-7 explains that a person who is double-minded (or also double-hearted as I have come to further understand it), cannot receive anything from the Lord. I used to read that verse "religiously" and misunderstand what was being said. I *mistakenly assumed* it meant that God would somehow withhold from a person who is double-minded, or worse yet - punish them, because they were not thinking right; were not believing in His will (remember, His Will does not ever contradict His Word. His Will and His Word are the same). Scripture says *that* person cannot *receive* anything from the Lord. It is not that God is withholding, it's that the individual's "receiver" is thwarted! Once I saw it, I was so relieved to understand He would not withhold from me!

Scripture says the double-minded person cannot receive from God. It is not that He is withholding, it's that the individual's "receiver" is thwarted!

A word picture comes to mind, which I hope will be helpful. Think of a knob on a radio. The knob/dial on the radio has to be accurately focused on the clear radio signal in order to receive what that radio station is offering. If it is caught between two stations, unfocused or divided in its placement, the result will be static, and there will be no benefit of receiving great music or programming. The broadcasting network is not withholding anything from the person who owns the radio, rather, the person who owns the radio is not focusing correctly! It would be goofy for us to say about our local radio station, "Well, it must not be the programmer's will for me to be able to get the music today."

When I got the news from the doctors in February, I made a decision to declare God's report (His healing verses and promises), and Word of Life over my situation, and over my body. I trusted He would watch over His own Word and it would not return to Him void, but would produce His good fruit and His good intentions, just like He says He will in Isaiah 55:9-13. This gave me a *"to do"* and also an *"instead of"* to be practicing rather than worrying. By "dialing in" on His Word, I was tuning my knob/dial and focusing it on "God's station". In those verses I just referenced it makes it clear God is inviting us to come to Him for help, and He watches over His Word and causes it to come to pass wherever it gets sent. I was leaning on His promises and He was the faithful Almighty Who would watch over His Word with His love on my behalf.

I DECIDED TO BE LIKE AN ARROW. Arrows shot out of a bow are committed! I was "set like flint" toward believing the report of the Lord (the healing promises), rather than the report of the doctors. Because of what Romans 10:17 says "faith comes by hearing...

the Word", I knew the more I saturated myself with God's report (Word), the more my faith would grow. In Isaiah 53:5 God's report says, "By His stripes, ye were healed," referring to the beating Jesus took prior to going to the cross. Psalm 103:1-5 reminds me to not forget all God's benefits. It lists them, and it's a great list: "Bless the Lord, O my soul; and all that is within me, bless His Holy Name! Bless the Lord, O my soul, and forget not All His benefits:

Who forgives all your iniquities,
Who heals all your diseases,
Who redeems your life from destruction,
Who crowns you with loving-kindness and tender mercies,
Who satisfies your mouth with good things, so that your youth is renewed like the eagles."

Faith-filled expectancy is fertile ground for miracles and answers to prayer!

I knew that "Bless the Lord" meant to approach Him with appreciation and praise for who He is. **I could open my mouth and do that whether I felt like it or not, even through tears.** I liked how clear and easy-to-understand the list of God's benefits was. *It instructed me to not let myself forget His benefits, because remembering them would do me great good.* It gave me something very healthy on which to build my faith and have a sense of expectancy. Faith-filled expectancy is fertile ground for miracles and answers to prayer!

I really liked verse 3 of Psalm 103 because it says, "He provides healing for all our diseases." Last time I looked up *"ALL"* in the dictionary, it means just that: *ALL! No exceptions.* I was encouraged by that. So despite a bad report from the doctors, I had recourse!

<u>Quick Scripture References - Chapter Two</u>

James 5:14   …anoint with oil, get prayer from elders NKJV
James 5:16   …confess your sins that you may be healed NIV
James 5:15   …if sick have sinned, will be forgiven NIV
Isaiah 53:5   …healed by the stripes of Jesus NKJV
Exodus 15:26b   …He is the Lord God Who heals us NKJV
Matthew 12:36, 37 …will be judged for our careless words NIV
I John 1:9   God is faithful to forgive us and cleanse us   NKJV
I John 1:8   …don't deny being a sinner…self-deceived…NKJV
Isaiah 26:3   …perfect peace…mind fixed on God… NLT
Isaiah 9:6   …a Child is born…Mighty God… NKJV
Matthew 1:23 …and you shall call His name Jesus…NKJV
Matthew 12:34 …out of …heart the mouth will speak…NKJV
James 1:6, 7   …don't be double-minded…can't receive NIV
Joshua 1:6-9   …don't let His Word depart from mouth…NKJV
Deut. 6:1-9   remembering His Word causes good success NKJV
Isaiah 53:5   …by His stripes we are healed….NKJV
Psalm 107:20 …He sent His Word and healed them…NKJV
Hebrews 4:12   God's Word is alive and powerful… AMP
Hebrews 13:8   Jesus the same yesterday, today, forever…NIV
Isaiah 53:1-5   What God accomplished through Messiah NKJV
Nehemiah 8:10 … joy of the Lord is your strength…NKJV
Psalm 16:11   …In His presence is fullness of joy…NKJV
Isaiah 55: 9-13   …God produces with His Word…NKJV
Romans 10:17   Faith comes by hearing…the Word…NKJV
Psalm 103:1-5   Bless the Lord, remember His benefits NKJV

CHAPTER 3

Tests, Tests, and More Tests

What time I am afraid, I will trust in Thee
Psalm 56:3 (KJV)

In THE ENSUING WEEKS throughout March and April, I went through a myriad of tests. Each test educated me more and more about what was going on in my body (which provided additional insights for focused prayers).

Two months prior to all this starting, my wonderful fourteen-year career with Toyota ended, due to many departmental cutbacks. That had been a very sad experience for me. After the downsize I decided to do part-time office work for a few months before starting the task of interviewing for another high-powered administrative job.

I could see that even being downsized was part of God's provision for me, because my medical tests were taking up so much time it would have been problematic for my career. I still had good medical coverage for a year, which covered the expenses for all the tests I was having, as well as the impending surgery. Working part-time freed me for all the appointments, and also gave me more time to be home alone during the day for quiet study, prayer, and deeper meditation on the healing Scriptures as I "fought the good fight of faith." I could see God's care even in these details. James 5:16 (AMP) had more meaning than ever before: "...the earnest (heartfelt, continued) prayer of a righteous man makes tremendous power available [dynamic in its working]." I noticed increased awareness being developed in me due to being in the Scriptures so much. It didn't leave any room for fear to get a foothold in my thinking.

A Careless Comment During an Ultrasound Test

While having an ultrasound test done on my left kidney, I got a lesson in "guarding my heart with all diligence" like it says in Proverbs 4:23 (the Amplified Version is particularly potent in its wording). Everybody at the hospital was nice to me each time I went in for tests, but this particular day there was an insensitive and careless comment made that offered an opportunity for me to become very discouraged, even angry.

As I lay on the table being scanned with the ultra-sound wand, the technician said, "I don't see anything. I can't find a thing. Why are you here again?"

Quite honestly, when she said that my heart jumped a little. I wondered if I had already received a miracle and the mass would be altogether gone! Hope soared in my heart as I lay there. I told her that a mass had been discovered on my left kidney, so the specialist had sent me over for the ultrasound.

She pushed a little harder with the ultrasound wand on my kidney area, still having difficulty seeing anything unusual on the screen.

She called a supervisor over with the comment "Can you try? I'm not finding anything."

I lay there waiting with baited breath, full of hope. Then the one commented to the other "Oooooh, there it is! Oh, wow, uhmmm, yeah, I can see why he sent her over. Look there, that's cancer for sure. It's *huge*, gosh...what a shame"... and her voice sort of trailed off softly.

MY HEART CRASHED WITHIN ME. I could not believe my ears! Not that I hadn't already been hearing that from every medical person I had dealt with, but I was stunned at the insensitivity in her comment. I was being talked about as if I were not in the room, as if I didn't have any feelings, and as if I were a hopeless case. Didn't they realize there was a *person* attached to the mass they were studying on the ultrasound?

Strife was being offered again, not directly through an argument, but this time incognito via something a technician in the ultrasound lab said. I had to refuse to let her words get to me, along with the fear that could have come with them. I had to guard my heart against that negativity, getting hurt feelings, or becoming bitter.

I was becoming more aware of how insidious strife could be, and this time I wouldn't let myself fall for it!

Fortunately, it was the only time out of all the times I went there in which that sort of thing happened.

It was disguised in a "different outfit" – a careless comment that brought hurt and discouragement – but there was that strife again, trying to find a way into my heart.

After hearing the comments of the supervising tech, I sort of shut down and got all numb feeling again while I was getting dressed. I walked out to my car, and before I put the key in the ignition, I started to cry really hard. I knew I had to let that hurt and anger go, and forgive the woman for her insensitive comment. Unforgiveness is dangerous; I surely didn't want it cluttering up my heart as I was trusting God for healing! The last thing I needed was for some root of bitterness to grab hold inside me. It had shown up disguised in a different outfit, but there was that strife again, trying to find a way into my heart. Would I fall for it this time? NO! I was learning to be more aware all the time.

I DEFINITELY HAD SOME TEARS THAT DAY as I drove home. It would have been easy to call a friend and rehearse what had happened during the appointment, venting about what had been said while I was lying on that table. But that would have fed the strife, like watering a root that was trying to get a chokehold within me. *I was not going to let that happen.*

I knew exactly Who would be appropriate for me to vent to, because I definitely needed to talk about it! On the drive home I cried hard like a little kid and tattled to God about what the tech said during the ultrasound.

I burst out with, "Heavenly Father, what she said hurt my feelings and felt scary. I felt like a pathetic piece of meat when she made those comments. I do NOT receive what she said about the mass. I am trusting You as my Healer, and that bad "c" word is certainly not part of my inheritance in Christ. You tell me in the first chapter of Ephesians that I have inherited every spiritual blessing in the heavens through Christ Jesus. *You don't pass out disease and cancer in Heaven to people!*

"Her words beat me up, Lord. I bring her words to You, and bring them under the power of the Name of Jesus, like it says to do in II Corinthians 10:4, 5. I trust You to protect my heart from what she said so it won't stick in my head. I cannot afford to receive any type of discouragement.

"It is written in Isaiah 54:17 (NASB) that 'No weapon that is formed against you shall prosper', and in Proverbs 26:2 it says '...a curse without a cause shall not alight', so her words have no life and cannot produce against me. Help me to forgive her insensitivity, Lord, because I am so angry and hurt right now I feel like I could just scream at her. Help me to let this go. I lay it at Your feet Jesus." I was very rattled, because I am not naturally good at forgiving when I get hurt, so I really knew I needed God's help.

Even while I poured out my frustration, I made sure my words were full of the Word of God, His Word of

Life, and I refrained from name-calling, which did admittedly cross my mind! When I got home, I opened up my Bible, and "took my medicine" by reading all the healing Scriptures out loud to myself.

Some people might think I was overboard in reading the healing verses to myself as often as I did, but I don't know of anything that would have been better or more productive in the face of being told I had cancer and was going to lose a vital organ! Numerous phone calls to friends to voice fear or worry wouldn't have helped me be fortified or courageous. I was choosing the healthiest thing I knew to do. The option I chose was to habitually fill myself with the words of life that would build up my faith.

The option I chose was to habitually fill myself with the words of life that would build up my faith.

I wanted a full arsenal to wage a counter-attack at the enemy that was attacking me, and I knew my biggest ally was God! I was not about to be passive or even on the defensive. Nope, I was taking the *offensive* with His Word! I was choosing to believe literally what it says in Proverbs 4:20-22 (AMP). I was taking those verses as the curing medicine from God to combat that mass inside me.

I personalized the verses as I read them out loud to myself: "My son (daughter Jackie), attend to My words; consent and submit to My Sayings. Let them not depart from your sight; keep them in the center of your heart.

For they are life to those (me, Jackie) who find them, *healing* and *health* *to all their flesh* (to every part of my body). Keep and guard your heart with all vigilance and above all that you guard, for out of it flow the springs of life."

To me, those verses weren't religious or difficult to understand, *they were just plain practical!* They told me how to apply the Word of God and what I could expect as a result. His Word is like medicine for the body, not just being limited to the soul (mind, will, and emotions) or the spirit. To me it was GOD'S anti-cancer treatment!

To me, the healing verses weren't religious or difficult to understand, they were just plain practical!
They told me how to apply the Word of God and what I could expect as a result.

How I Handled My Emotions

THE TWELVE WEEKS OF WAITING prior to the surgery, along with the discouraging x-rays, would get to me sometimes and I definitely did some crying occasionally. I was tired of being told each test indicated cancer. I did not want my kidney to get cut out of me! I didn't want a big scar that wrapped around half my torso. I did not want to have to go through chemo.

I talked out my feelings to God: "Father, I need to let the tears flow right now to get some of the pressure out. I know You love me; I know You're good. I know You are powerful, I know You are ALL Mighty, not 'Some' Mighty! I know Your Word stands forever because

53

Isaiah 40:8 (AMP) tells me so and *You* are my Rock. In Mark 13:31, Jesus said, 'Heaven and earth will pass away, but My words will by no means pass away', so I know You are the Answer, and all of Your provision for me is *in* Christ. I know that, I just need to be Your little girl right now and cry."

I focused on what His Word tells me, instead of my emotions. Even with tears and feeling scared, I made sure my mouth proclaimed God as my source. I said, "I know" in each sentence because I was establishing between Him and me that I know these things about Him. I don't wonder, I *know*. God says we should remind ourselves to focus on His benefits (Psalm 103:1-5), so I did that in prayer whenever I needed to.

I focused on what His Word tells me, instead of my emotions. Even with tears and feeling scared I made sure my mouth proclaimed God as my source.

I would **PRAY THE WORD**, rather than pray about how scared I was. I already knew I was quite scared. Rehearsing that to God would not build up faith in me! *I needed faith and trust, not rehearsal of the fear.*

I was praying the solutions, rather than the problem!

It wasn't fear-based or 'wishing-for' praying, it was promise-based, *covenant-based* praying. I literally prayed God's words over myself. That was how I knew I was praying His will. God's Word and His will are one. Jesus said He and the Father are One, and John 1:1 tells us "In the beginning was the Word, the Word was with

God, and *the Word was God.*" Then John 1:14 tells us "The Word became flesh and dwelt among us." Jesus and His Word are One. God and His Word are One.

I would PRAY THE WORD, rather than pray about how scared I was. I already knew I was quite scared. Rehearsing that to God would not build up faith in me! I needed faith and trust, not rehearsal of the fear.

The medical procedures made me feel uncomfortable or scared sometimes, so I would remind myself fear was not an option! II Timothy 1:7 (AMP) tells me, "For God has not given us a spirit of fear, but of power, and love and a sound and well-disciplined mind." I would also remind myself God promises to never leave me nor forsake me (Hebrews 13:5). In Isaiah 43:2 (KJV), He reassures us and says, "If you pass through the waters, they will not overtake you, and if you pass through the fire it will not kindle upon you." Those are powerful promises. This tells us that in spite of circumstances or conditions that would normally overwhelm us, if we stay consistently focused on Him, we will see His power and know His Presence.

I would tie my heart to a promise that addressed what my issue was; doing that protected my mind, gave me peace, and helped my entire body respond better to the treatment because I was peaceful. It was another *promise in action:* "Thou shalt keep him in perfect peace whose mind is stayed on thee" (Isaiah 26:3 KJV). Sometimes a nurse gave my hand a squeeze, or put a kind hand on my arm to reassure me. That touch was heaven-sent. If you are reading this and you are in the medical profession, a kind word and human touch is huge in those moments to a person who is scared and having tests. When a nurse or technician reaches out like that, they are truly being used by God as an ambassador of His kindness and comfort. They're like angels!

I would tie my heart to a promise that addressed what my issue was; doing that protected my mind, gave me peace, and helped my entire body respond better to the treatment because I was peaceful.

I'D HAD TO WAIT SEVEN WEEKS to get in to see the specialist I wanted to meet with for that "third opinion" I was seeking...that was a lot of time to wait...and to keep anxiety away. I wanted somebody to tell me what I wanted to hear – that it was not cancer! I wanted to hear doctors and technicians change their minds and stop telling me that they were 99.9% sure that the mass on my kidney was cancer (they saw cancer every day for a living and my x-rays had "cancer" written all over them). I wanted *somebody* to tell me something that would give me hope!

I had to face it - I wasn't going to get that "good word" from the medical side of all this. The explanations of why the kidney had to be removed were logical; it would have been very easy for me to receive those conclusions into my spirit. If I had done that, my heart would not have been "good soil" for God's Word to grow in, and produce answers to my prayers. It could have changed my focus to begin to believe that there was no "win" in my situation - that they were right, and I would have to lose my kidney. No miracle can land on that kind of thinking!

The x-rays could have changed my focus to begin to believe that there was no "win" in my situation - that they were right, and I'd have to lose my kidney, but no miracle can land on that kind of thinking!

Rebel Cells

God is not overwhelmed by the report of doctors. He is the God who can change the DNA of cells. During my journey, I kept meditating on any Scriptures that would confirm His power and "bigness". It helped me keep focused during tests at the hospital. I thought about what the verses in Philippians 2:9-11 (NASB) tell me about Jesus: "Therefore also God highly exalted Him, and bestowed on Him the name which is above every name, that at the name of Jesus every knee should bow, of those who are in heaven, and on earth, and under the earth, and that every tongue should confess that Jesus Christ is Lord, to the glory of God the Father."

I realized cancer is a *name*! So I told myself that "c" word would have to bow its knee to THE "C" word, which is Christ Jesus! That realization helped me a lot. Jesus' Name is highly exalted and is *THE* Name which is above every name. It gave me a picture of cancer bowing to the power and Lordship of Jesus Christ. It also gave me a visual of His Name being in my body like a pacman from the original computer video games - pursuing and swallowing up cancer cells anywhere they might be in my kidney or elsewhere.

I realized cancer is a name! So I told myself that "c" word would have to bow its knee to THE "C" word, which is Christ Jesus!

One day after coming home from more tests, I was struggling and tearful about everything. Seeking His help, I asked the Lord, *"WHAT IS CANCER TO YOU?"* As quickly as I had finished that question I was startled with a lightning quick response, and I was also struck by the tone of the response. I got an answer, but it was clearly as if something very inferior was being mentioned, as if it was no big deal at all. The answer that came lightening quick back to my heart stunned me because it had the tone of contempt to it.

His answer was, *"Rebel cells."*

REBEL CELLS! Of course! From God's perspective, cancer wasn't scary... it was rebel cells - cells that were growing wildly on their own, outside of His plan. It was rebel cells not following His design of replication, whether they were in the kidney, the liver, the blood, the brain, it didn't matter. It was cells rebelling against His perfect and orderly design.

Suddenly I knew how to approach them - not with fear, but to see them from God's perspective. After all, each and everything I was reaching for *had* to be from His perspective. *Healing was His perspective*; it certainly wasn't the doctors'. My perspective was too small, too limited, too easily overwhelmed by the medical reports I was getting, and the doctor's perspective was to cut me open and cut out an organ. God's perspective was definitely the one I wanted, and had to have as my source.

Cancer was cells rebelling against His perfect and orderly design.

Based on what God's Word tells me, I could copy Jesus and talk to those rebel cells. Cancer sounded scary, but rebel cells made me angry. Appropriately angry, righteously angry, "I-belong-to-God" angry! I could copy what Jesus tells us to do in Mark 11:23 and I could "speak to the mountain and tell it to be removed."

In my situation, the "mountain" was being told I had cancer. *If I had the nerve and boldness to* **copy and obey** *Jesus* and **DO what He said I could do**, then I could command those rebel cells to die in Jesus' Name, and I did! (Jesus taught in Matthew 7:24-26 to be <u>do-ers</u> of the Word, and not hearers only, and that is backed up again in James 1:22-25).

I could command those rebel cells to die and not take any good healthy cells with them. I could tell them that my body was the temple of the Holy Spirit, and they weren't permitted to use my body as a host in which to grow!

I could command those rebel cells to die and not take any good healthy cells with them. I could tell them that my body was the temple of the Holy Spirit, and so I did!

<u>Quick Scripture References – Chapter Three</u>

James 5:16b   heartfelt prayer of a righteous man avails…AMP
Proverbs 4:23   keep my heart with all diligence…NKJV
II Corinth 10:4, 5 .. bring every thought into obedience…NKJV
Isaiah 54:17   No weapon formed against me…NASB
Proverbs 26:2   A curse without cause will not alight…NKJV
Proverbs 4:20-22   God's Word is health and healing…AMP
Isaiah 40:8   God's Word stands forever…AMP
Mark 13:31   Jesus' Words will never pass away…NKJV
Psalm 103:1-5   …forget not all His benefits…NKJV
John 1:1   …the Word was with God….and was God   NKJV
John 1:14 …Word became flesh, and dwelt among us…NKJV
II Timothy 1:7   …not given fear…but a sound mind…AMP
Hebrews 13:5   I will never leave you nor forsake you…NKJV
Isaiah 43:2   tough or scary times, God will help, protect…KJV
Isaiah 26:3   perfect peace if keep mind on the Lord…KJV
Phillip. 2:9-11   Name above every name…NASB
Mark 11:23   say to the mountain, don't doubt in heart…NKJV
Matthew 7:24-26   hear and DO His teachings…NKJV
James 1:22-25   DO the word, not just hear it…NKJV

*   *   *

CHAPTER 4

Fasting Along the Journey

"...Consider carefully what is before you;
And put a knife to your throat
If you are a man given to appetite."
Proverbs 23:1, 2 (NKJV)

The surgery date was approaching quickly. I wanted to cleanse my body internally, so I fasted from certain foods. I also trimmed wasteful use of my day, always looking for more time to meditate those healing verses.

I let go of consuming sugar. I suddenly saw it as an enemy of my body. My awareness about food had intensified as a result of what I was facing. Apparently cancer loves sugar in the body, so I didn't want to give that nasty "c" word any fuel. A lover of chocolate and sweets, which were abundant at the office almost daily, I taught myself to re-define those foods as "not-kidney-friendly" and it helped me walk away! Brownies, donuts, and sweets were the enemy!

Deep down inside I knew that I probably had that mass growing inside me because of my own poor eating habits and appetites. That is the main reason I never said, "Why me, God? Why did this happen to me?"

Truthfully, over the previous 20 years I had eaten enough junk food, especially chocolate, to destroy a bull elephant's kidney and knock him over in his tracks! I wanted to take as much responsibility as I could while looking to God as my Healer. I faced the truth that my eating habits had been nothing short of abuse of the body that I had been blessed to live in. I had been very negligent in taking care of it. Blessed with a tall, athletic-looking body, I looked okay on the outside, but *I had been abusing my insides* for years! Immediate lifestyle changes were necessary - I decided I would eat more vegetables than usual, add more fish than chicken, and lessen red meat to once or twice a month, plus drink water, water, water! Better late than never.

I went on the internet and read articles about natural ways to help cleanse the kidneys and the liver. I learned a warm glass of distilled water with two tablespoons of virgin olive oil and a fresh lemon squeezed into it before bed was a wonderful way to naturally cleanse those organs as the body goes into rest and fasting mode for the night. I discovered that fresh lemon is a natural bacteria fighter.

I learned that all purple foods (grapes and plums, pomegranates, purple grape juice, boysenberries, blueberries, etc.) are very good for the kidneys, the liver, and the gallbladder. Those foods purify the blood, which then refreshes those organs. They are natural cleansing and healing foods, especially if organic.

I also started learning about wheatgrass and drank it fresh each day. I discovered Jamba Juice carries it and makes it fresh upon request. I learned to not take it with the slice of orange chaser, because the citrus dilutes the natural healing potency of the wheat grass. Everything I read about it told me it had tremendous value as a healing food. It was another source of living, healing, *wisdom food* from my Creator, and I was determined to do all I could on every level to minister to my body.

I scrutinized how I used my time. Unless something was absolutely necessary, it got set aside. I had to go to work, of course, but television went by the wayside, so did reading magazines and chatty phone calls; all were set aside for one main purpose - to glean more time for meditating on God's Healing Word. The kind of input I allowed myself to receive would help keep my spirit as uncluttered as possible.

I thought about people who had to hold down a full-time job, plus had a family, and might be facing the same type of ordeal I was facing. I recalled ways I redeemed time when I was still raising my kids, holding down a 40-hour a week career and going to school two nights a week for another degree. I made study tapes for myself and listened to them while driving the freeway and running errands. The same could be done to meditate the healing verses. Making a tape by reading all the healing verses into it and listening is highly effective. We tend to be drawn to the sound of our own voice and will pay more attention!

There are many ways to creatively make time for the Word of God to build ourselves up. Scripture says that if we will diligently seek Him with all our heart, all our soul, and all our might, He will let us find Him, and He *will* answer us. (It does not say we will "get more religious" - it says we will literally find God!)

I took on the attitude of a focused athlete who has to hold down a job, but also wants to prepare for the L.A. Marathon. Many years ago a co-worker friend of mine named Lynette challenged herself to run the L.A. Marathon. She studied what it would take to prepare and complete the course. I watched for months and was amazed at her focus and discipline! Every day she got up at 4:00 a.m. to run two training hours before she got ready to come into work. She also ran three training hours each evening after she got home, and she demanded of herself six to eight hours of running both days on the weekends.

Her example challenged me! If she could do that to prepare for a marathon, I could certainly prioritize my time to "fight the good fight of faith" and dig into the healing verses to get healed from a report of cancer! No, I didn't get up at 4:00 a.m. to read the Scriptures the way my friend did to run and train for the marathon, but I did re-order the use of my time to pursue *my* priority. **Nobody called her a fanatic or over-the-top.** She was appropriately focusing to reach her goal.

The parallel was clear to me - I was in a marathon of sorts myself and wanted to approach "race day" (my surgery coming up on May 3) and come out on the other side whole and sound, with TWO kidneys, despite what all the medical facts indicated would happen.

Lynette and I talked about how she made herself train *whether she felt like it or not.* She talked about "hitting the wall" in those final weekends in which she would make herself run 20 miles without a break to ready her body for the race. She was building stamina. She said sometimes every step mocked her and taunted her with, "Why am I doing this? Am I nuts?" but she wouldn't listen to that. She kept her eye on the prize, to be able to complete that marathon on race day!

To me, everything I was doing was building faith stamina. I was devoted to my Coach (Jesus and the Holy Spirit) and His instructions (the Word of God) so that everything in me could be lined up to receive the healing which Christ had already provided for me through that beating He endured prior to going to the cross.

Isaiah 53:3-5 (AMP) explains, "He (Jesus) was despised and rejected and forsaken by men, a Man of sorrows and pains, and acquainted with grief and sickness; and like One from Whom men hide their faces He was despised, and we did not appreciate His worth or have any esteem for Him. Surely He has borne our griefs (sicknesses, weaknesses, and distresses) and carried our sorrows and pains [of punishment], yet we [ignorantly] considered Him stricken, smitten, and afflicted by God [as if with leprosy]. But He was wounded for our transgressions, He was bruised for our guilt and iniquities; the chastisement [needful to obtain] peace and well-being for us was upon Him, and with the stripes [that wounded] Him we are healed and made whole."

Everywhere in those verses that it says "our" or "us", I mentally put "my" and "me" and received it deliberately and personally, using it as a prayer of thanks. I read those verses out loud repeatedly, focusing slowly and thoughtfully, pondering each line as if I were searching for gold. That is what "meditating" the Scriptures is...It is *far more* than a casual read.

It was like God was saying
"This work of healing I did in my Son when He took
that beating for you...it's a SURE thing!"

I Corinthians 1:30 (KJV) says, "...you are in Christ Jesus, who became for us wisdom from God...". God is saying that *Christ is* made unto me His wisdom! **All the wisdom of God is IN Christ – *it's packaged within Him,*** because He is the Word of God made flesh, the Word in an "earth suit" - and part of God's wisdom was healing, **because He had provided healing for me *in* Christ, *by* Christ, and *through* Christ.**

This was plainly explained and emphasized with a "Surely" added to the beginning of verse 5 in Isaiah 53. It was like God was saying "This work of healing I did in my Son when He took that beating for you... it's a SURE thing!"

That was a way better report than the one I was getting from the oncologists! I was going after *life* on behalf of my kidney! I was learning to recognize and shun death in any subtle forms of negativity or anxiety. I was choosing life in how I thought and spoke, changing how I thought about food and what I would and would not eat, and most especially I was choosing life by being in the Word of Life as much as possible.

We all know the phrase "You are what you eat". Poor eating habits produce poor health. That is applicable in a parallel illustration regarding the Word of God, and faith versus unbelief. *We will become what we let influence us.* Daily life bombards us with negativity. We know the phrase "garbage in, garbage out", referencing what we put into our minds. I didn't listen to any doubting people say, "God doesn't heal anymore," or "It isn't His will to heal everybody," – because it wouldn't help me have any confidence toward God to ask for healing!

I fueled myself on "what Papa says" (God's Word) as my steady diet, knowing faith would grow, and confidence toward the goodness of God would increase a boldness to believe. I figured it was up to me spiritually to daily fill up on God's Word, the same way it was up to me to do way better in feeding my body responsibly for maximum healthy results. It was a clear parallel.

I also looked for ways to amputate any doubt, unbelief, or traditional thinking that could hinder or deplete my faith in Him.

Quick Scripture References - Chapter Four

Isaiah 53:3-5   healed by his stripes...AMP
I Corinthians 1:30   Christ made unto us wisdom...KJV

CHAPTER 5

God's Moving

"The Lord will perfect that which concerns me..."
Psalm 138:8 (AMP)

It was mid-April, the seven-week wait to see the third specialist had arrived. I brought my ever-growing set of x-rays and reports so the whole medical history was available. He and I reviewed the progression of x-rays from the last nine or 10 weeks, beginning with the first one from the emergency room back on February 23rd.

What he said stunned me. "When you closely compare the x-rays over the last two months, it is DEFINITELY GROWING."

That was *not* what I had wanted to hear! Then he said, "See how a month ago in this x-ray it was this size, but in this more recent x-ray it's larger and the side of the kidney is now bulging out slightly?"

Bulging out? I did not want to hear *that* either!

He quickly followed with "But this is interesting. **The mass appears to be moving slightly.**"

What did he mean appears to have *moved slightly*? I leaned in while he showed me what he was talking about. It was bigger, but it had slightly relocated itself! I was seeing something on the x-ray which, at least to me, meant prayer was being answered. The mass was no longer as centrally located over the part of the kidney that produces urine, hence allowing the possibility for the kidney to function properly. Even though the doctor didn't say so, to me this meant it might now be more operable...

In His ministry, Jesus spoke to circumstances (the raging sea), things (the fig tree), even demons, and when He did, powerful things happened.

I Talked to That Mass!

The x-ray showed the mass was changing. On the way home in the car I was giddy! I told God I would continue to trust Him, regardless of what I saw, but it was surely great to finally hear and see something that I could interpret as encouraging.

In His ministry, Jesus spoke to circumstances (the raging sea), things (the fig tree), even demons, and when He did, powerful things happened because He spoke with His faith-filled words. I figured if I copied Jesus like a little child, I couldn't go wrong! Scripture says He has given His followers authority to use His Name. So, I spoke *TO* that mass and rebuked it! I told the mass it was NOT allowed to grow in my body, and that it could not prosper against me or do me any harm, in Jesus' Name. I knew I was authorized to declare that because of Isaiah 54:17, "No weapon formed against you shall prosper."

When Jesus experienced being tempted forty days in the wilderness, He had a head-on confrontation with the devil. He handled each blow the devil threw at Him by saying, "IT IS WRITTEN", refusing each temptation and distraction of the enemy, and using God's very words (Matthew 4:1-11, AMP). Jesus would quote Scripture, and let God's Word do the fighting for Him! So, I copied that and shouted, "IT IS WRITTEN 'By the stripes of Jesus I was healed' according to Isaiah 53:5."

I spoke to that mass and rebuked it! I told the mass it was NOT allowed to grow in my body, and that it could not prosper against me or do me any harm, in Jesus' Name.

I was full of hope and asked God to continue to protect the health of my left kidney from the mass.

I raised my voice and said, "Mass, you die in Jesus' Name, and you will not steal any of my healthy kidney cells. You will not take my left kidney in Jesus' Name!" Yes, I was fired up all right! I was pretty boisterous in my car as I drove home. I didn't care who saw me!

Some people may be reading this and think, "Lady, you're a fruitcake, talking to your kidney, and talking to a mass growing in your body!" People may think I'm a fruitcake, but I got my miracle, and I know *God's Word is living and powerful, and produces results!* (Hebrews 4:12, AMP)). I know He is faithful to watch over His Word and it will not return to Him void! (Isaiah 55:11).

People may think I'm a fruitcake, but I got my miracle, and I know God's Word is living and powerful, and produces results!

An Astonishing Moment in My Driveway!

Earlier I said I went from one doctor to another, to get a second, third, and even fourth opinion. I kept hoping someone would tell me something I *wanted* to hear! As I arrived home from the medical center and was pulling into my driveway, something powerful clicked in my understanding. I'd just finished telling that mass it couldn't have my kidney, when something started to stir in my heart. I felt as if a geyser-like energy force of understanding was about to explode!

I remembered the verses I had been reading the day I got that first phone call -- the verse that said, "O LORD my God, I cried to You, and You have healed me. You have kept me alive, that I should not go down to the pit (the grave)." (Psalm 30:2, 3, AMP).

As I pulled into the driveway, another verse was coming up strongly. It was Isaiah 53:1, **"WHO HAS BELIEVED OUR REPORT, AND TO WHOM HAS THE ARM OF THE LORD BEEN REVEALED?"**

Scripture was "talking" to me, directing my thoughts, guiding my faith, teaching me, and revealing insight. It was not me remembering a Bible verse. That verse was being quoted *to* me, inside my heart. It was as clear as when I sensed God telling me to focus on *His* words during that initial phone call in February when Dr. Lowe told me I had to be prepared to lose my kidney.

Lights went on inside my understanding like high voltage electricity. It was a shift in understanding. My own thoughts were not just thinking of a Scripture; rather my understanding was being quickened with a significant insight.

His Word had a VOICE!

It was not me remembering a Bible verse. That verse was being quoted TO me, inside my heart.

I realized God was asking me a question through time and space through that verse in Isaiah 53:1! There was a force to it. I realized in that verse He was asking *anyone* who would listen, from the very first time He ever spoke it all the way through history to me at that moment in my driveway! He was asking, "WHO has believed Our report, and to whom has the arm of the Lord been revealed?"

It hit me so hard! A verse I had read many times went from simply being words on a page to a living question that was personal to me! It had a "voice". No, I *don't* mean I was hearing voices, it was just suddenly alive to my heart. I was *getting it*! (Proverbs 6:22 says God's

Word will lead us, keep us, and **when we wake, it will** *speak with us*).

God only asks you a question because He wants to get you the answer!

I had been going from doctor to doctor hoping somebody would tell me what I wanted to hear, and suddenly The Somebody was telling me something I wanted to hear! It was Somebody Himself! It was coming in question-form through that verse. Like my pastor says, "God only asks you a question because He wants to get you the answer!"

IT WAS QUICK, LIKE LIGHTNING ANSWERING LIGHTNING, because the question came to my spirit, and it was my spirit that answered back in a flash. It was much faster and more powerful than me just thinking about something. I was excited! I hollered out, "I'm the 'Who', God. *I will*! I'm the 'Who' that will believe Your report! I believe it, Lord! I believe You! The answers are from YOUR mouth. Your report is the report I need and where I will put my focus!

"I won't get it going from doctor to doctor, or from specialist to specialist, hoping one of them will tell me something that makes me happy. *They* can't make that mass go away! They can't make it change and not be the 'c' word. But YOU can! I'll take Your report Lord, because Your report is the Truth."

Then it hit me; His report really is THE Truth! I was experiencing one of the most profound "Aha!" moments of my entire life! It was high voltage insight, but with good results to bring healing!

The second half of the verse was the rest of the question to my heart: **"...and to whom has the arm of the Lord been revealed?"** I felt like I was going to burst out of my skin because I was getting it! I hollered back to the second part of the question in that verse at the top of my lungs: "I'm the 'to whom', God! It has been revealed to me! *I get it!* The 'arm of the Lord' has been revealed to me! I know His Name! His Name is JESUS! The Arm of the Lord is Christ JESUS! He is Your Arm of strength and power and provision *to* me and *for* me! I get it, God! I *see* it!" I am not the least embarrassed to tell that by this time I was crying as I was yelling out my response to Him, but crying with excitement and deep humility too, because I was getting it. I was amazed, thrilled, and grateful.

Years ago I saw the movie "Contact" with Jodie Foster and Matthew McConaughey. In the storyline, Jodie Foster was a scientist and astronomer who followed her passion, researching for years trying to discover if there was any intelligent life out there in our solar system or beyond. In the movie, her dedicated efforts were rewarded with some amazing discoveries and *deeply personal encounters.*

One of my favorite scenes in the movie was when she finally realized there was a live "read" on the tracking screen of her computer...and it was coming from outside our galaxy. She had a *transforming moment* where she suddenly understood the pattern and the communication that was being sent. She almost busted out of her skin with excitement...

Well, *I* was having *my* very own "contact" moment, so-to-speak, right there in my car, on my driveway, and it was equally transforming for me! It wasn't on a scientific computer screen picking up messages from other galaxies like in the story-line of the movie, it was happening in my heart and understanding as insight was coming to me "live" out of Scripture.

I too thought I would burst with excitement! I have heard preachers say, "*One word from God, when it comes alive to your understanding, has the power within it to set your heart free and turn your situation around.*" I was experiencing one of those moments. I knew God was communicating to me through His Word and He was defining Himself as my champion and HEALER!

I thought it was remarkable that God used the Word "report" in that verse. That verse was close to 2,700 years old; it was prophetically spoken a good 700 years prior to Jesus being born! I realized God has been asking that question throughout the generations, hoping people will listen and receive as He sends out the answer from His heart. **He is always looking for people to whom He can transmit His light and wisdom. He is always looking for willing hearts that will receive!**

His wisdom was saying to my heart: "I AM your doctor, I AM YOUR HEALER. *I* am your Great Physician. Believe MY Report. The doctor is giving you a report that puts fear in your heart. *I* am giving you a report that puts life, hope and power in your heart. Instead of believing reports of humans who are doing their very best, (but even at their best they are practicing medicine), instead **believe ME!"**

Then the next part that came to my heart really amazed me: "I AM not practicing, I AM your answer. I AM the I AM. Say My Name and fill in your need. I AM your Need-Meeter! I Am your Source, your Provision. I meet your need! I AM the Almighty! I AM your All-in-all."

It was as if I had the doctors' reports in my left hand, and then I had "the Report of the Lord" out of His Word in my right hand, and God was asking me WHICH REPORT would I choose? Which report was I going to *bank on*? I was amazed. Familiar verses were coming alive inside me. I was pretty choked up to think that God was making Himself so real to me. A flood of verses came bubbling up in my heart and bathed my mind, washing fear away and giving clarity –

John 1:1 and 4, also verse 14, "In the beginning was the Word, and the Word was with God, and the Word was God ...In Him was Life, and the Life was the Light of men" and "the Word became flesh and dwelt among us" (Jesus is the Word!).

Psalm 107:20, "He sent His Word and healed them and delivered them from their destruction."

Malachi 3:6, "For I AM the LORD and I do not change."

Hebrews 13:8, "Jesus Christ the same - yesterday, today, and forever."

God was connecting verse after verse together and releasing the power of His answers and solutions into my understanding. I was being dowsed in living love, power, and answers! Heaven's wisdom was being downloaded into my spirit. Maybe I was in a medical storm, but God's Spirit was anchoring me securely in the power of His Word.

I quickly responded with, "The doctors' reports and the x-rays may be the medical facts, God, but You and Your Word and Your Provision are THE TRUTH." A hush of deep stillness came over me as that settled in my understanding. I was awe-struck.

The difference between the two was suddenly crystal clear. I would have been a fool to be in denial about the medical issues going on in my body, or to go around chanting the words, "I refuse to have cancer, I refuse to have cancer, I'm not sick, I'm fine," as if it were some hopeful, positive mantra! That would have had no substance, and would also have been medically irresponsible, as well.

Maybe I was in a medical storm, but God's Spirit was anchoring me securely in the power of His Word.

The facts were definitely clear all right, and I *was* being medically responsible by going to every single appointment, having all the tests needed as I prepared to face an apparently necessary surgery. I love medicine and science. They are extremely valuable and God has provided both to us. I was using medicine as a tool in His hand, trusting Him as my Source. Doing that in no way meant I wasn't applying trust in His Word. Doctors know how to cut us open and stitch us back up, but bottom-line, Who teaches the cells to knit back together? The way I see it, *it's all God!*

I would have been a fool to deny the medical issues going on in my body, or to go around chanting, "I refuse to have cancer, I'm not sick, I'm fine," as if it were some positive mantra! That would have had no substance, and also been medically irresponsible.

The more deeply I meditated on the healing promises, the more I was learning that there is something (or should I say Someone) that is greater than medical facts: THE TRUTH, which IS the Word of God, backed by His Name and all that He is. We say we believe in a living God, so logically, it was reasonable that He was responding to and providing me these insights because of all the time I'd put into pursuing *Him*! Understanding came because I was continually seeking Jesus' help, grace, power, strength, peace, and healing through His Word. The insights came like brilliant flashes of light.

Scientists tell us light travels at 186,000 miles per second. In John 1:4 it reveals about Jesus, "In Him was Life, and the Life was the Light of men." These flashes of insight came like bursts of light-filled understanding, and they were faster than I could think!

This was not something I was talking myself into, this was something that was alive and grasping *me*! In theological terms it's called RHEMA. There are Greek words used to describe the Word of God. One such word is "Logos", which means the written Word itself, what we know as the Scriptures on the pages. Another word is "Rhema", which means *"living* word" or *"revealed* word". It is when a particular verse jumps off the page and becomes alive in our understanding by the Spirit of the Living God. It is that electric "Aha!" moment I was talking about. It was God getting through to me and it left me feeling astonished and thrilled!

Quick Scripture References – Chapter Five

Isaiah 54:17 No weapon formed against you...NKJV
Matthew 4:1-11 Jesus uses Scripture to resist the devil!...AMP
Isaiah 53:5 Healed by His stripes...NKJV
Hebrews 4:12 The Word is alive and powerful...AMP
Isaiah 55:11 ...His Word will not return to Him void ...NKJV
Psalm 30:2-3 I cried to You and You have healed me...AMP
Isaiah 53:1 God asks: Who has believed Our report...NKJV
Proverbs 6:22 God's Word will speak *with* you...NKJV
John 1:1, 4, and 14 In the beginning was the Word...NKJV
John 1:4 ...in Him is Light...He is the Light of men...NKJV

*   *   *

CHAPTER 6

The Dream Prior to Surgery

"He was bruised for our iniquities...and
by His stripes we are healed".
Isaiah 53:5 (NKJV)

The impact of the committed study, meditation, and
keeping my heart and mouth tied to God's Word began
to run deep; it produced some powerful things in
unexpected ways.

One night I had an amazing dream. I was drifting up to
wakefulness from deep sleep, but I think I was still
dreaming. In the dream I saw something I could not
readily identify. Staring a little harder, I began to realize
I was looking at a person - a man. He was horribly
messed up and looked hurt to the point of being almost
unrecognizable as human. He was hunched over on his
knees, dressed in some sort of a cloak which was torn in
shreds. The closer I looked, the more I saw in detail,
like a camera that was focusing from blurry to crystal

clear. He appeared filthy dirty, not from being unbathed, but from being horribly beat up. Then I realized he wasn't dirty - what appeared to be dirt was actually a lot of dried blood.

He had long hair that was loose, tangled all around his face, and matted with blood. I couldn't see who he was. In the dream I cautiously walked in a wide circle to the right to see better, while still keeping a distance, because I felt alarmed at what I was seeing. He was hunching over something, and his arms were wrapped around it. His head was bowed protectively over it as well. As I looked more closely, I could see he was hunched over a person, protectively wrapping himself around them.

THEN I REALIZED WHAT I WAS SEEING. He was acting as a human shield for the welfare of the person he was protecting. As I looked more closely to see who he was protecting, he started being beaten again. I watched, while tears streamed down my face, because I caught a clear glimpse of the person who he was protecting from the horrible beating, blow upon blow. The person being shielded was me.

I suddenly knew that the man in my dream was Jesus, and He was taking that beating that was meant for me upon Himself, on His own back – the beating of brokenness, sickness, disease, and …of cancer. I was stunned to the core with how much He loved me and to what an extreme that love had taken Him! In the form of a dream, I was privileged to see an intimate explanation of the verse in Isaiah 53:5, "He was bruised for our iniquities… and by His stripes we are healed."

Healing passages I had meditated on were illustrated to me in this profoundly personal dream. Having difficulty recognizing Him as human in the dream also lined up with Scripture, because it says in Isaiah 52:14 "Just as there were many who were appalled at him — his appearance was so disfigured beyond that of any man and his form marred beyond human likeness." (NIV)

I began to understand that Christ had *already* met my need according to the detailed explanation in the entire chapter of Isaiah 53. I had greater clarity and understood that the blows on His back were cancer and every other known disease, sickness and death. He had taken those diseases for me already, substituting Himself *for* me. He had become my provision, so that centuries later when disease came at me to try to destroy me, I could <u>know</u> that *He had already provided Himself as the answer* for protection and healing for me.

I began to understand that Christ had already met my need according to the detailed explanation in Isaiah 53.

MY BACK FOR YOUR BACK

He was showing me, *"MY BACK FOR YOUR BACK."* He was saying to me, "I did this for you. I AM Your Protector and Provision. I AM your Healer. **I AM your healing**, I AM your Shield. You don't have to *ask* Me to be, because *I already AM.* You don't have to ask Me to heal you, because I already HAVE through Christ as I fulfilled prophecy. *Pursue receiving what I have already accomplished for you.*"

I was beginning to understand I didn't have to try to convince Him to heal me. I could be sure when I prayed in His Name His willingness had already been thoroughly accomplished, as fulfilled in Isaiah 53.

Doctors tell us the beating Christ took from those whips (the cat 'o nine tales as it's called) ripped chunks of flesh out of His back that went all the way into His lungs, kidneys, and liver, as well as the muscles that surrounded the ribs.

They say most people never survived even half way through a Roman scourging because it was intended to kill. Jesus stayed alive through that beating to fulfill the promise of being the Word that was sent to heal us, as it says in Psalm 107:20: "He sent His Word and healed them, and delivered them from their destructions."

Jesus stayed alive through that scourging in order to *then* go to the cross to pay for our sins - and to also be the prophesied Great Exchange of Righteousness for our *un*righteousness. He provided forgiveness for our sinful waywardness from God and His ways, and Christ alone is our way *back* to God. If we ask, He will fill us with His own Spirit to give us the power to live our lives to honor God.

That powerful dream stayed with me for days. I hardly spoke. It stunned me into wonderment. The Lord didn't have to be so kind to show me something like that and visit my heart in a dream!

His Word was enough. His promises were enough. But He answered my prayers and in a very personal way opened up my understanding! I was truly amazed and humbled.

I realized that just as God had carved out His covenant of the Ten Commandments on the tablets of stone for Moses to give to the children of Israel, so also He had carved out His covenant of healing for humankind on the back of His own Son...to be forever available to meet the needs of every generation yet to come.

Quick Scripture References – Chapter Six

Isaiah 53:5   by His scourging we are healed...NKJV
Isaiah 52:14   His appearance was marred...NIV
Psalm 107:20   He sent His Word and healed them...NKJV

CHAPTER 7

Surgery Day

*"I shall not die but live, and will proclaim what the
Lord has done"*
Psalm 118:17 (NIV)

ON THE DAY OF THE SURGERY I was blessed to
have my family wait with me as I waited to be taken in
and prepped for the procedure. My husband, parents and
brother were there, and my daughter Erica had flown in
from Pittsburgh. My son David was over in Scotland,
playing in NFL Europe, so he wasn't Stateside. My dear
friend Janeen had generously forfeited a vacation day to
be off work and be there at the hospital with me super
early in the morning before I went in for the surgery.

I was escorted by a nurse behind those big, grey doors
that led to surgery; everyone had to leave for work and
would return later, but Janeen stayed all those hours of
the surgery to wait with my mom and keep her company.

She hadn't wanted my mom to be alone if the doctors came out with bad news. That was so precious!

I was paranoid about any mistakes being made on my body, so I had taken a permanent-ink blue marker and written on myself a big X and the words, "Not *this* kidney, the *other* one!" over the right kidney area! (Surgery was to be done on the left kidney.) Weird, I know, but hey, haven't we all read about the bizarre mishaps that occasionally happen in hospitals? I didn't want to be one of those statistics!

When I was getting "gowned up" for the procedure, the nurses saw what I had done on my body with the marker, and they giggled. But then they did the neatest thing - they handed me an even brighter *purple* marker, and they said "We use purple for our patients, so would you please mark yourself with this purple marker as a double precaution so the doctors know *we* did that here with you?"

I thought that was wonderful, and it made me feel so safe that everyone would take good care of me while I was under the anesthesia.

As I was wheeled down the hall toward surgery I started to feel pretty vulnerable, so I comforted myself and began to quietly sing, "My Jesus, my Savior, Lord there is none like you..." It is a song from Hillsong ministry that I really love. I hadn't taken any of the pre-meds because I am so overly sensitive to anesthesia as it is; it is not good for me to combine one med upon another, or else it takes nine or ten hours for me to wake up from a surgery. Because of not taking the pre-meds I was somewhat nervous, and very alert!

I looked up from the gurney in the surgery room and saw the nurses, the anesthesiologist, and my "heroes", Dr. Baghdassarian and Dr. Shanberg.

I asked everybody's names with the comment, "It's absurd to me to let people cut me open when I haven't even been properly introduced to them!"

They all chuckled, but we did introductions, even though I couldn't see what they looked like very well because of their blue shower-cap-looking head covers and surgical masks. I could hear a smile in their voices behind their masks, and most importantly, I could see their eyes. I told them I was a little scared and asked them to wait a minute before they put me under, so I could pray for all of them to be very skilled and for their hands and abilities to be blessed by God on my behalf. Yes, I did that, right there on the spot! I had no doubt WHO I wanted to be sure was in charge of that surgery!

When I said, "Amen," the anesthesiologist was so awesome and said, "Jackie, we will take good care of you, and I will give you the champagne princess treatment."

I said, "Okay, I'm ready."

They started the drip of the anesthesia, and I don't even think I was able to count to three before I was totally out.

Right after the surgery was completed, while I was being taken to recovery, Dr. Baghdassarian went out to see my family and friends in the waiting room to let them know I had come through just fine, and got to keep the kidney! The next ten days would prove if the kidney would be able to function or not after having such a large part cut out of it. He explained the tumor had an unusual molecular structure, but they were confident it *was not cancer*. Photos of the tumor were taken for my file. He said the photo probably would be used for a medical journal for students to study. He said it was pumpkin colored, quite large, with unusual cells.

After the surgery, Dr. Baghdassarian went out to see my family in the waiting room to let them know I had come through just fine, and got to keep the kidney!

When I started "coming to" in the recovery room, I was aware of one only thing: excruciating pain! It was severe, all around my upper left chest and especially in my left shoulder. I woke to hearing my own voice hollering at an embarrassing volume, asking for help to make the pain go away. Someone came over - I kept crying out in an almost panicked manner. I told them I felt like I was having a heart attack. They asked me where the pain was and then they explained it was the gas from the surgery that was traveling through my body and was trapped in my shoulder. Gas? Did I hear that correctly? I was groggy, that didn't make sense to me, I started to cry and begged them to please make the pain stop. I don't know what they gave me, but I gratefully slipped back into the comfort and escape of deep sleep.

I awoke a second time feeling someone shake me gently, asking me if I knew my name. I didn't hurt nearly as much in my shoulder, although I had overall sensations of periodic shooting pains that were piercing.

They told me I was still in recovery, and explained the shooting pains I was experiencing were from all the gas that had been used during surgery to extend my abdomen.

Apparently during a partial wedge nephrectomy the abdomen is extended to become pretty large, creating room so the doctors can move about in the torso to get to the kidney! They said the gas travels through the body, sometimes getting trapped in joints and between the abdominal organs as it dissipates... and can cause a great deal of discomfort (no kidding!). I was told it would take about twenty-four to forty-eight hours to work its way out of my body. They asked me how I was feeling otherwise and told me to try to start to stay awake because they wanted to take me to my room so my family could see me (that sounded good). *Then they congratulated me and told me I had gotten to keep my kidney!* Music to my ears! I smiled, whispered groggy praise to God, and drifted back to sleep.

Quick Scripture References – Chapter Seven

None listed in this chapter.

CHAPTER 8

After Surgery: Gratitude

"Give thanks to the Lord, for He is good; for His
mercy and loving-kindness endure forever."
Psalm 136:1 (AMP)

I had severe nausea for the next two days, struggling to even keep water down. That was very rough to deal with, having just had such a major surgery done through my abdomen. Vomiting is one of my least favorite things in the whole world! I had fasted two days *prior* to the surgery to be sure my system was completely empty. This was to protect myself from the possibility of vomiting while under anesthesia and causing possible bronchia aspiration, which is very dangerous. The wretching and dry heaves after my surgery was awful and lasted on-again, off-again for hours at a time. I was so hungry, and so empty, now having gone four days without food. They couldn't get the queasiness to stop, even with medicine. The gas and anesthesia just had to work themselves out of my body, and I would have to endure being along for the ride with all those unpleasant symptoms, which added to the soreness from the surgery. I cried a little, but I had no complaints, even with all that to deal with, because I was STILL A TWO-KIDNEY WOMAN!

When they closed me up after the surgery and I found out I still had two kidneys I knew I'd been given a miracle. I remained in the hospital three days, and then went home to continue to recover. I asked to be taken straight to the church before going home and being put back in another bed. I was so grateful surgery had gone well and I had two kidneys. I had quiet tears running down my face, and all I could say was, "I want to go to church."

I asked to be driven to the church where I'd originally had the elders pray for me when all this had first started. I knew it would be open and easy to get into, plus it was only a mile from my residence.

I shuffled my feet slowly with tiny painful steps down that long aisle to the front of the church. Moving and walking hurt, plus I had two very long clear tubes protruding out of my body (they were necessary for another two weeks so the internal surgery area had a way of draining and a "read" could be done on the contents of what was draining out of me). The tubes hung down at my side and were taped along my leg. At the bottom they were connected to a large draining pack, all of which was discreetly tucked into a large purse-looking bag that I could carry low at my side so no one could tell or see the tubing or the drainage bag.

I struggled to drop to my knees when I got to the front of the church, and literally sobbed the words, "Thank You" over and over for a good twenty minutes. Even though I was uncomfortable and had many weeks of recovery ahead of me, I knew I had been spared a great deal. God could see my heart. Sometimes tears are powerful worship. Each tear contained deep gratitude. They were words enough.

Sometimes tears are powerful worship.

The first four days at home I gratefully slept most of the time because my abdomen was really sore and I was fairly weak. I needed help to be able to move at all or change position for sleeping, having no torso strength to turn my body, or lift and shift my own legs. Getting in or out of a bed was impossible without support and help. Each movement was very painful for the first five days at home. Gradually I gained some strength to move on my own. Finally managing to balance and bathe on my own felt like a triumph!

A nurse came every other day to check the tubes to be sure the kidney was draining and recovering, take my vitals, and be sure I didn't have any fever, which would have indicated infection. She would also change the dressing over the three-inch incision site just left of my navel. I trusted God for a good recovery, the same way I had the entire time prior to the surgery. The biggest issue we were waiting on was if the kidney was recovering well enough to produce urine after having such a significant part cut away from it, and would there be less blood showing up in the tubes each day, which would mean all was healing well deep inside the kidney.

I was back in Dr. Shanberg's office about ten days after surgery for my follow-up with him. He told me it had been a stellar surgery, and the final biopsy on the extra kidney tissue had shown clean. **I was happily pronounced cancer-free by the doctor!**

I gave him a hug and told him thank you. He took a moment to admire the stitched incision areas and check to be sure they were healing properly. A nasty raised area of scar tissue was forming in the largest incision area by the navel, but I knew I would be talking to God about that and believe for it to become nice and flat, smooth, and pale like the rest of the skin, (which it did within a year).

The doctor walked out of the room and his assistant came in and said she was going to pull the tubes out of me.

I said "What? Wait! *Wait*! I get a numbing shot or something before you do that, right? And don't you guys need to be using antiseptic stuff and stitching me up or something? How much is this going to hurt?" (From the first appointment to the last, I was never a passive patient! I asked questions about *everything*, and was my own advocate at all times!)

To my surprise I was not going to be given a shot, and I was also not going to be stitched up!

The tube was as big (wide in circumference) as a large-sized Starbucks straw or a straw for a thick milkshake, so I was a little freaked, to tell the truth!

To my protesting "But, but, but..." they simply said, "It will be fine, lie down, take a slow deep breath, try to relax and get a focal point."

They helped me lie flat (my abdomen didn't get back to total normal ability or strength to freely move without help until three weeks after surgery) and they began to pull out the tube. I thought that weird "there-is-an-alien in-me" feeling would never stop! It didn't hurt at all, but it *did* feel really creepy. It felt like they were pulling as much tube OUT of me as what was already hanging out of my body! When they showed me all the tubing that had been inside me I was really surprised.

When I looked at my abdomen, I had a hole big enough to stick my pinky finger into where the tube had been hanging out! "I have a hole in my body you guys! Fix it, close it up, this is creepy!" I said.

Dr. Shanberg explained the hole would close up on its own, and it wouldn't scar.

"Are you *kidding me*?" I exclaimed. "But it's bigger than the size of a dime - you can't just leave me like this with a hole in my abdomen! Won't it get infected, with cooties being able to get in there?"

He chuckled and told me it would close up beautifully. They just taped a gauze patch over it and told me to not get it wet for about five days. I was flabbergasted. Sure enough, he was right. The hole closed up on its own, and the cells knit together without producing a scar! It gave me another reason to admire God's handiwork. Where "man" did the stitching, there were marks and scars, but where God did the "knitting together" of the tissue, there was not a mark! Truly we are fearfully and wonderfully made and His code for healing is programmed right into our cells!

Quick Scripture References- Chapter Eight

None listed in this chapter.

*   *   *

CHAPTER 9

Reminiscing About The Journey

"My help comes from the Lord, the Maker of
heaven and earth."
Psalm 121:2 (NIV)

The surgery scheduler for Dr. Baghdassarian was a woman named Judy. I trusted her from the first moment I met her. She was very kind every time I came for an appointment with Dr. "B" as I prepared to go in for the surgery. I had talked openly with her about my faith and trusting God. She knew I was believing for God to change the tumor and nullify the cancer, and also to preserve my left kidney.

After the surgery, Judy and I had occasion to see one another about every four months for my follow-up exams with Dr. "B". We did a lot of rejoicing when the results came back from my surgery! I would always make a point to go into her area to take a few minutes to say "hello." I asked if she could make time for us to get together outside of the office for a visit. I had let her know I was endeavoring to write about my experience and asked to talk with her to see if she could help me with some information.

She was excited and very encouraging when she first found out I was going to be writing this book. She commented that my story and faith had impacted her powerfully and believed it would be an encouragement to others as well. She was willing to let me take notes while we talked, so I could accurately note her comments and anything she shared with me.

As we began our visit, I asked Judy if I had ever told her what happened when I went to see the third specialist prior to the surgery. I told her about the rollercoaster moment I'd had with Dr. "Y" (the third-opinion specialist I'd had to wait seven weeks to get in to see) as we looked at my x-rays together. He had commented the tumor was definitely getting larger, and of course, at the time my heart sank. But he also had commented he could see it was bulging out more to the side, as if it were moving away from the center. I told her that was a comment I had clung to, because I believed God was at work making changes for me that would cause the tumor to be more operable and help me keep my left kidney.

Judy and I recalled that initially when I came to see Dr. Baghdassarian, the x-rays all showed the mass was *centrally* located in the kidney and so the kidney was doomed either way. She remembered that as well. Hearing Dr. "Y" say it looked like it was moving from its central location a little was music to my ears. He thought it was a curiosity... I hoped I was on my way to a miracle.

Two months prior to the surgery, I had heard about a Dr. Shanberg, who was a well-known teaching surgeon at UCI at the time. He also happened to be a colleague of Dr. Baghdassarian and they shared an office together in another part of town. Although he was not a doctor available on my insurance plan, I knew the out-of-pocket cost to consult with him was an investment in myself. I'd been told he was one of less than a handful of surgeons in the western United States who had perfected doing the partial wedge nephrectomy. That meant rather than creating a cut that involved half my torso to get to the kidney (creating a scar from the navel all the way around to the mid-back), he could make a small incision next to the belly button, bypass all the intestines, and do surgery on the kidney through the front of the body. This would produce a much smaller three-inch cut at the navel, plus two or three half-inch sized incisions through which other instruments would pass. Needless to say, I wanted to meet him for a medical consult!

I told Judy about my first meeting with Dr. Shanberg. I had brought the x-rays from the other specialists so he could review them. As we talked in his office, he said he was sorry, but the tumor looked cancerous. He wouldn't tell me 100% that it was, because he could not know 100% until he got in there, but he said he was 99% sure it was cancerous and felt the kidney would need to be removed. He said he believed I was under great care with Dr. Baghdassarian and as long as Dr. "B" was confident it hadn't spread anywhere else, he too was confident I would be fine with one kidney.

As I talked with Dr. Shanberg, I explained my stance on believing the healing verses in the Bible and I was asking God for a miracle. He was intrigued with my perspective and belief that the power of God in the healing Scriptures could impact cells.

He told me he enjoyed working on people with strong faith because they tend to do well in surgery. He said they often heal more quickly and sometimes have less scarring. I told him I remembered articles that had come out years before in Time magazine featuring just that same topic.

As Judy and I continued our visit recollecting all the events leading up to and around my surgery day, I told her while talking with Dr. "S", I got bolder and pressed in to explain what I hoped for from him. I told him despite what all the tests and x-rays verified, **I was believing for a miracle** – for God to move powerfully on the tumor to *not* be cancer and also to get to keep my left kidney. I asked if he would cut with caution with an approach to save it, rather than automatically thinking it would be necessary to take the kidney out.

He explained to me the danger of cutting too near a cancerous tumor. He explained doing so would increase the possibility of splitting off the cancer cells, actually spreading it by not getting it all. He said it would be better to just remove the kidney.

As we talked he was respectful and appreciative of my perspective, as well as my hope that it wasn't cancer. He cautioned me gently but strongly, reminding me that he and all the other specialists believed from their findings it *was* cancer.

"I realize you are hoping for that one percent...but the professional consensus is the kidney will have to come out," he said.

He was very caring and said he did not want me to be disappointed or have it hurt my faith. He reminded me this was what he did for a living, twice a day, four days a week, for the last thirty-three years, and as a specialist he saw it every day. He felt confident I would come out of the surgery fine, that I was young, strong, and in good health overall.

"I'm sure you will do just fine and live a normal, happy life with the one kidney," he said.

I remained tenacious, and assured him my faith would not be shaken no matter what the outcome. I told him, "I will do what *I* do, which is trust God. I will trust God to do what *He* does, which is heal and give miracles. I will trust you to do what *you* do in being a top surgeon. It's a win/win! *I just ask that you go in with the idea of 'Let's see if Jackie got her miracle,* and all we have to do is remove this tumor and repair what is left of the kidney.'"

As Judy and I continued our visit, she jumped in and said she thought it was pretty amazing that I had been that bold with Dr. Shanberg. She also thought it was cool he took the time to listen so respectfully, assuring me he would take my perspective into consideration as he approached the cutting process.

I nodded, and continued telling her what I said to him next. I told him, "Obviously, if you get in there and find cancer, I'll trust your judgment to cut out anything and everything you decide needs to go! I just don't want you to go in there *assuming* upon the compiled medical evidence alone. **I believe God's power can supersede medical evidence**. I would like you to leave room for my miracle and rather go in with my perspective in mind initially, cutting with caution. Are you willing to do that for me?" I asked.

Judy's jaw dropped and she said, "Oh my gosh, Jackie, I can't believe you were that bold!"

I told her he gave me a big smile and kindly agreed he would approach the surgery from my perspective. I told Dr. "S" I was even willing to risk two surgeries if we could keep the kidney and give it a shot at recovering from the shock of what it would have to go through. I figured if it didn't start producing urine and show it could function as a kidney because of the trauma, we could go back in a second time and take it out!

"Jackie," Judy replied, "you need to remember, this is a doctor who is a *renowned* urology surgeon. He has thirty-three years of expertise in kidney cancers. *Every doctor confirmed, based on the evidence on your x-rays, it was their belief what they were seeing was cancer.*"

I told her as Dr. Shanberg and I concluded the consult, we shook hands on it! It made me feel great to know he would partner with my already trusted Dr. Baghdassarian and they would be a team for my surgery. What especially mattered to me was how respectful he was about my perspective of faith. He said he would write a couple letters on my behalf to my insurance carrier to see if he could get on my surgery team. I was so pleased, because normally he wouldn't be participating in my surgery, since he wasn't my doctor and wasn't a listed physician on my insurance plan. I left his office feeling very encouraged and full of anticipation!

Judy said she had seen the letter Dr. Shanberg had written to Dr. "B" in my file.

She commented "Your file is one of the thickest, most detailed ones we have in the office, Jackie."

There was another factor which showed God's hand working on my behalf, and to this day has remained a bit of a mystery to me. In the weeks prior to the surgery, I'd had to make many phone calls to my health insurance provider to push for permission to have the partial wedge nephrectomy, rather than the standard style of kidney surgery.

Initially they had been quite resistant, because it was a highly specialized surgery, and thus it was far more costly. But on the last call I made to them they noted that a doctor had written to them on my behalf saying he recommended I be allowed to have that surgery, *and he would help cover the cost.* They wouldn't tell me the name of the doctor, but said it was not anyone I named to them as we spoke. To this day I have wondered who that doctor was, but his influence and generosity helped my case. It was another one of those "humbled into grateful silence" moments as I wondered, "How did God do that for me, and who was that doctor?"

Judy said after my surgery, the other doctors and staff back in Dr. Baghdassarian's office who saw the photo of the tumor couldn't believe how *big* it was! She told me the biopsy report came back declaring the tumor to be *benign* and it was so amazing to all of them!

She said, "I felt stunned relief and joy for you, Jackie. *"Nobody could believe it* and comments were flying from office to office between the doctors. As tumors go, yours was *big*!"

She said Dr. Baghdassarian couldn't believe it, nor could Dr. Shanberg or Dr. Lowe; they were all stunned it was benign, because it showed *all signs* of being cancer.

Dr. 'B's' partner in the office had seen some of my x-rays too, since they had all discussed them. Judy had kept him abreast of my case because he had shown concerned interest. He too said **he couldn't believe it was benign, based on the myriad of prior evidence.**

As Judy and I sat there talking and I was jotting down what she was sharing with me, I kept saying, "Really? *Really?* I never realized they all talked about it that much."

She said everyone on staff had taken an interest, especially since I was trusting so much that God would intervene. She said she had tried to have hope for me, but they were all completely convinced they were looking at cancer the whole time, x-ray upon x-ray, especially because of the way it was growing. She said that was why they were all so surprised after the surgery - and it thrilled my heart afresh all over again with renewed gratitude.

I told Judy what a family member had said, "Maybe it was cancer initially, but with all the prayer and being in the Word, God had hovered over His promises, gone in there, given me my miracle, changed it at the cellular level, and protected me and my kidney! Maybe it had such an unusual molecular structure because it *had* been changed from cancer to something else..."

I thought that was a dear comment and an interesting perspective - one I was quite comfortable with because I believe the Word of God is watched over by His power and love, and will bring healing. I told her I believe God's words are so pregnant with power they can literally change the DNA of something. It can go inside and impact at the cellular level. I think that is where I got my miracle – at the cellular level.

Judy commented she sees so many people come through the office who will need surgery, and all too often their outcome is not as remarkable as mine. She had some questions about people who believe in God and don't get healed.

I believe the Word of God is watched over by His power and love, and will bring healing. I believe God's words are so pregnant with power they can literally change the DNA of something.

We discussed what Scripture tells us about Jesus in His own home town, "He could there do no mighty works because of their unbelief." (Matthew 13:58). I explained that doubt can show up in many disguises which will block a person from receiving from God. I also shared how the heart can want to believe but the head can be full of wrong teaching, thus causing conflict, crushing the ability to trust and receive.

Doubt, in its many disguises, will block receiving from God. The mind can be full of wrong teaching, thus causing conflicted thinking and crushing the ability to trust and receive.

I said, "If people have been in a church that has filled their heads all their lives with statements like 'Well, the gifts have passed away,' and 'God doesn't heal people anymore,' it is hard for people to believe and trust God for something that they think He does not do anymore! They will not think they can ask Him for much of anything! They have actually been taught to be double-minded and thus doubting, when they approach God, and it says in James 1:6, 7 that person '...will not be able to receive anything from the Lord.'"

Judy could see there is no basis for confidence when someone's head is full of conflicted beliefs.

I said, "If the Word of God isn't taught, there is no confidence in God's mercy or generous heart. If people are not in the Scriptures for themselves, they have no vision to receive a healing. Even God says 'My people are destroyed from lack of knowledge' in Hosea 4:6."

I mentioned factors that can hinder faith. Many people don't want to deal with the fact that Jesus Himself taught there is a devil who does evil. Essentially the devil is the terrorist of the spirit world. He hates us simply because we are God's creation and object of His love. Jesus talked frequently and openly about the devil, saying He came to undo the devil's works. Jesus would heal the sick, undo diseases, and set people free from tormenting spirits. This clearly indicates those things are the devil's will for humanity, NOT God's, or else Jesus would not have "undone" them! That is just deductive reasoning.

If people are not in the Scriptures for themselves, they have no vision to receive a healing. Even God says 'My people are destroyed from lack of knowledge' in Hosea 4:6.

As Judy and I wrapped up our very significant time together, she mentioned there was *one thing above all else* that really impacted her as she watched me go through the cancer-scare journey. She said she marveled at it *then* and *still* thinks about it frequently on behalf of other people. She said she asks herself, **"What would it be like to have that kind of faith?"**

I told her it is a matter of asking for wisdom (just like Scripture tells us to in James), and then holding on to God's Word with pit-bullish tenacity. It also involves making a decision to know and believe the Lord's promises first and foremost, and to pray the Word of God over the situation, knowing He is all-powerful, faithful to His own Word, and willing to be full of mercy.

Then it's a matter of doing what comes to the heart's understanding (as long as it is in line with God's Word) and trusting with an uncomplicated acceptance that God is good and will watch over His Word to cause it to produce, as it says in Isaiah 55:11.

Quick Scripture References – Chapter Nine

Matthew 13:58 unbelief of the people hindered Jesus...NKJV
James 1: 6, 7   have faith, don't waiver or won't receive...NIV
Hosea 4:6   Lack of knowledge destroys *God's* people...NKJV
Isaiah 55:11   His Word will produce whereunto it's sent...NKJV

*   *   *

CHAPTER 10

A Second Chance to Believe

"Trust in the Lord with all your heart, and lean not to your own understanding"
Proverbs 3:5 (NKJV)

My surgery had been on May 3. About two months later, just as I was getting stronger and had started back to work, I had a follow-up x-ray done on the left kidney to see how all was healing internally since the operation.

I got a call from Dr. Baghdassarian asking me to come into his office to review the x-rays. There were some things on the film again in the left kidney area that he wanted to talk about with me.

We called them "blips", but he said we needed to watch them, because it looked like the tumor might be doing a re-growth, and if it continued, I might have to lose the rest of the kidney.

I was rattled to the core. Not again, not *again*! I was very discouraged for two days, and then I got a grip on myself and asked, "Lord, what do I *do*? I don't get it. I have come this far, *You* have brought me so far, and now *this*? **What do I do, Lord?**"

I was like that for several hours off and on with a general "fogged" feeling in my head and heart. I shook it off, and prayed again, and this time when I asked, "What do I do now?" I was impressed inwardly with a question: *"What did you do the first time?"*

I knew what the answer was right away. It was *always* going to be the same answer: *GO BACK TO HIS WORD.*

I felt beat up. I felt discouraged. I felt frustrated, and I didn't want to "go back to the drawing board". I wanted it to be easy from here on out, and I realized it might not be. I felt overwhelmed, BUT, I put myself back in His Word, I made myself worship, and I got very busy reading the healing verses all over again to my kidney. I also got really mad at the devil, told him he did not get to steal healing from me, and reminded him of the verse in Isaiah 54:17. I copied the way Jesus answered him in Matthew 4 and I said, "IT IS WRITTEN" and then I aggressively quoted Isaiah 54:17, "No weapon forged against you will prevail, and you will refute every tongue that accuses you. This is the heritage of the servants of the Lord, and this is their vindication from me," declares the Lord. (NIV)

Everywhere that verse said "you", I put in "me" and "I" to have it fit and be personal. I also reached for Isaiah 54:14, 15 with a loud, "IT IS WRITTEN, 'In righteousness you will be established: Tyranny will be far from you; you will have nothing to fear. Terror will be far removed; it will not come near you. If anyone does attack you, it will not be My doing; whoever attacks you will surrender to you.'" (NIV)

I needed to hear that, **I wanted the devil and fear to hear it, and I wanted my kidney to hear it!** Yes, I felt like crying, but that was my emotions. Maybe I wanted to cry, but even through tears I could still make my mouth and heart reach for God's Word and apply it as God's living shield on my behalf, despite my emotions.

Along the way in this entire journey, ONE OF THE MOST VALUABLE THINGS I LEARNED was *my emotions had nothing to do with faith.* I might be crying so hard sometimes I would have nose-bubbles like a little kid, but as long as I was clinging to God's Word, I was still in faith and **my emotions had nothing to do with whether or not His Word was powerful or would work on my behalf.** That was a relief to learn!

Maybe I wanted to cry, but I could still make my mouth and heart reach for God's Word and apply it as God's living shield on my behalf, despite my emotions.

It wasn't up to me to "huff and puff and have enough faith". No, that's a lot of pressure! The focus was to be on Him, not me trying to be adequate enough or some "faith giant". Happy or sad, feeling brave or scared, I could still open His Word and read it out loud; even through tears I could still open my mouth and praise Him, trusting Him to watch over His Word to cause it to

113

produce, as He promises He will do (Isaiah 55:11). *My emotions, tears, or fears didn't diminish God's bigness or power!*

I took myself to the local church again because it was so close to home, and I knew I would have easy access to the pastor. At Sunday a.m. service I told him what was going on...that new x-rays showed "something" on the left kidney again, and the doctor wasn't sure if the area might be creating a re-growth of the tumor. Pastor suggested I come back at 5:30 p.m. for the prayer meeting prior to the evening service. He said I could meet with those folks and get prayer. I was very grateful.

My emotions, tears, or fears didn't diminish God's bigness or power!

When I came back that evening per his suggestion, the pastor met me outside the little classroom where the prayer team met. About fifteen people were there. He brought me in and introduced me, because none of them knew me, since I didn't regularly attend there. He suggested I fill them in on what had transpired since February 23rd, and bring them up to date (it was now July, two months since I'd had the surgery on May 3), and tell them what had just recently shown up *again* on the follow-up x-rays.

I shared with them about the unshakeable-ness of God's healing Word, regardless of circumstances. I brought everyone up to speed with a quick history, and then I said, "I would like prayer, but I am going to be very specific and tell you that I *don't* want anyone to lay hands on me please unless you are very confident of the Word, and that it IS God's will to heal, and specifically to heal ME. I don't want anyone to pray for me and say things like 'Oh God, if it be Thy will to have Jackie have cancer, please have her deal with it bravely for Your Glory', because that is not praying *God's* Word, and hence His will over me!"

"If you can't agree with what I am asking for, that is okay with me, just please don't touch me. I would like you to have full freedom to be honest about where you are and what you may believe, but this stuff is too serious and I cannot have unbelief spoken over me. I only want you touching me with prayer if you can agree with God's healing promises in faith, nothing wavering, because I need the power of agreement prayer. Jesus said, 'If any two of you agree as touching anything, it shall be done for them of my Father which is in Heaven.' He didn't say 'hope for' or 'wish for', He said '<u>Agree</u>'."

The pastor just smiled at me, because he was used to my boldness. Then to my surprise he walked out of the room, and those folks were all left looking at me with big eyes. God bless him for giving me such liberty!

The people gathered around me, and only two people put their hands on me. The rest stood around in a circle, and many of them put their hands on the two people who had their hands on me. Only two people prayed for me, while the rest were quiet, but I knew in my heart they were doing their best to agree in faith with the two people they knew who *did* pray. It was really special, and very honest before one another and God.

One of the people who prayed said simply, "Lord, you see this woman's faith. Do for her what she is asking and believing." That really struck my heart because it was just like Scripture.

The other person simply said, "Lord, I agree with that prayer, and we trust you to be strong on Jackie's behalf and honor Your own Word."

I was thrilled, and I knew that was all it would take, because Jesus taught if two or more people agree in prayer, their prayer will be answered!

I hugged lots of people and told them thank you so much for allowing me the freedom to pour out my heart, be so blunt when they didn't know me really at all, and for their love and grace to pray for me and show me kindness.

As I was walking outside to my car, two people caught up with me quickly and said "We have never heard anybody talk or think the way you do! How did you learn to be so aggressive with trusting God's Word?"

I habitually ask God to give me holy boldness to believe His Word.

I shared a little of my background in learning the Word, and encouraged them to be aggressively dedicated to study the Scriptures for themselves daily so it could bear powerful fruit in their own lives. I also told them I habitually ask God to give me holy boldness to believe His Word, so I can honor Christ as much as possible in

116

how I think and believe. We had a great time together, encouraging one another and talking about God. It was wonderful and meant a lot to me.

Within another two months the shadows that had showed up on my left kidney were gone. Thank You Lord!

<u>Quick Scripture References – Chapter Ten</u>

Isaiah 54:17   No weapon formed against me will prosper   NIV
Isaiah 54:14, 15 ...terror shall be far from me...NIV
Isaiah 55:11   His Word produces wherein it is sent ...NKJV

CHAPTER 11

His Power Has No Limits

"For the eyes of the Lord run to and fro throughout the whole earth, to show Himself strong on behalf of those whose heart is loyal to Him"
2 Chronicles 16:9 (NIV)

Doctors study and devote themselves to bring healing through medicine. They are intensely dedicated people. They do their best to meet medical challenges and find answers to help people get well. They define what the medical facts are so we will know what we are dealing with (and we can pray more accurately!)

I was learning that the power of the Truth (God's Word) is even greater than circumstances. God's Truth has the power to supersede medical facts. Facts are subject to change, but Truth is eternal and unwavering.

The best way I can convey what I am saying is to draw a parallel, using the example of GRAVITY versus the LAW OF LIFT. Gravity is a scientific "given" and considered a natural law. That is why it's called the *LAW* of Gravity. It is a fact that forever stands. The Law of Gravity is in full effect 100% of the time on planet earth! Wishful thinking will not make the Law of Gravity go away. Saying it isn't there (denial) won't make it go away either. None of that has power or substance.

God's Word, Power, and Truth are like the Law of Lift.

Anyone with a pilot's license or who understands aerodynamic physics knows there is a principle known as the Law of Lift which *can* and *does* supersede (or overpower) the Law of Gravity. The Law of Lift was *always there*, waiting to be tapped into. The Creator taught birds to apply what the Wright brothers had to discover! It was there all the time!

The Law of Lift supersedes the Law of Gravity every time a plane lifts off from the ground to successfully take flight. As irreversibly present as gravity is, it can be superseded, or overpowered, by a greater principle - a *greater* law in physics. God's Word, Power, and Truth are like the Law of Lift.

Things that we call supernatural (healing, for instance) are just normal to God. In His Word, He constantly invites us to "come up higher" in our thinking and understanding (read Isaiah chapter 55, AMP). Scripture says He is Light. When we pursue Him through His Word, He is more than willing to "enlighten us" about Himself.

The medical facts I was dealing with were like gravity: very real - but the power of God's Word was definitely germinating in my understanding and I received revelation that the TRUTH of God and His Word was like the Law of Lift – it could supersede the 'law of gravity' or the medical facts I was dealing with. It could and would overpower them.

Being in Faith While Using Medicine

When I use the term "bookending", it is a word I came up with for the visual picture I get when I REACH FOR GOD'S HEALING POWER. When hit with medical issues, or a need for medical help from my doctor, I see the medical help as one part of a bookend set, and the Scriptures and "Sword of the Lord", which is His Word, as the other side of the bookend set.

Another way to describe this is to take your right hand and call it God's Word, take your left hand and call it medical assistance. Now, with palms facing each other, bring your hands together. Your hands are like two bookends, meeting in the middle. When I say I "bookend" the issue, the physical need is in the middle, and I "hit it from both sides" to get the need met.

I avail myself of medical help if I need it, but I understand that GOD MY SOURCE has been kind to make that available to me for my use and advantage. It is God, not the medical staff, who is my power Source at all times. For example, I can swallow medicine, but WHO helps the cells respond to it? Doctors can cut us open and stitch us back together, but WHO teaches the cells to knit together again so our insides don't fall out? **His WORD is like the Law of Lift that carries me to His answers being fulfilled on my behalf**, but as I wait on Him I also have complete liberty to get medical assistance and not waiver within myself thinking I don't "have faith". Every bit of it is framed by trust in God, His Word, and His goodness.

THERE WAS A DAY IN MY LIVING ROOM WHEN I REALLY NEEDED HELP grabbing faith from the Word.

I was discouraged, so I was praying and worshipping, and said to the Lord, "Lord there is nothing greater than a crucified Jesus being raised by Your power."

The thought quickly came back to me, "Yes, there is."

It startled me. I wondered if that was not God, but the enemy. It didn't seem like God would say something like that to me.

I said, "Lord?" What floated up next in my heart was surprising to me.

"Turn to Ezekiel 37. Jesus had been dead three days, but *His body was still in tact.* **I want you to begin to realize just WHO you are dealing with!** *I am so much bigger than you yet realize.*"

I opened my Bible and studied Ezekiel 37. This is an astonishing account in which a prophet was shown a giant valley full of bones from skeletons of fallen warriors. The bones had been there so long they were scattered randomly all over the place and were bleached stark white. The prophet asked the Lord about the bones, and an amazing interaction began to take place between him and the Lord.

God asked the man, "Can these bones live?" (which must have seemed like a preposterous question!)

The stunned prophet answered, "Oh Lord God, You know."

(I am guessing he felt like saying, "Heck no!", but he had the good sense to realize he was in the presence of the Almighty, Whose power is without limits. I think his answer was concise, safe, and very wise!).

God is so much bigger than we reason Him to be.

After the prophet answered, "Oh Lord God, You know!" God told <u>him</u> to *speak the words of God* TO the circumstances to make something happen. The key to think about is that *GOD* didn't speak to the existing circumstances; He instructed *the man* to do the speaking!

The key to think about is GOD didn't speak to the circumstances; He had the <u>man</u> do the speaking.

Ezekiel 37:4-7 says, "Then he said to me, Prophesy to these bones and say *to* them, 'DRY BONES, HEAR THE WORD OF THE LORD! This is what the Sovereign Lord says to these bones: I will make breath enter you, and you will come to life. I will attach tendons to you and make flesh come upon you and cover you with skin; I will put breath in you, and you will come to life. Then you will know that I am the Lord.' So I prophesied as I was commanded." (NIV)

God told the prophet, "*Say to* these dry bones 'Live!'"

When my journey began, God had directed me to speak TO my kidneys and tell them to "Hear, receive, and obey the Word of the Living Lord Who created you", and then I would read the Scriptures about healing (the words of the Sovereign Lord) to my kidneys several times a day.

It was dawning on me that what God told *me* to do regarding my kidney actually matched Scripture more closely than I knew! I just figured since Jesus talked to things (fig tree, wind, waves, sea, and dead people) it was reasonable the Holy Spirit had directed me to do the same. At the time when He was directing me to do this I wasn't even aware of Ezekiel 37, so I didn't realize He was having *me* do something He had instructed a prophet to do probably well over 3,000 years ago in the face of impossible circumstances!

I was directed to Ezekiel 37 because I had been sitting on my couch trying to encourage myself by worshipping God, and because I had said, "Oh Lord, there's nothing greater than a crucified Jesus being raised by Your power." The Lord wanted to make me aware of something even more "beyond impossibility" than Christ being raised after being dead in the tomb three days. **God was "connecting the dots" for my understanding once again to show how extraordinary He is.**

While praying and seeking for the Lord to strengthen my faith after another discouraging test result, He surprised my heart with, **"I want you to begin to**

understand just WHO you are dealing with and how powerful I AM!" *Through Scripture He wanted my "awe-ometer" to get a better grip on how far-reaching and limitless His power is.*

The magnitude of what God accomplished in Ezekiel refreshed my faith once again to realize any medical report I was faced with was *not* going to stump God!

I pondered the magnitude of what God accomplished in Ezekiel 37 and my faith was refreshed once again to realize any doctor report I was faced with was not going to stump God!

Scripture defines Jesus as THE WORD in John 1:1 and in Revelation 19:13 as well. In II Chronicles 16:9, Scripture tells us that God's eyes search the earth, for those on whose behalf He can show Himself strong.

God's generous, merciful, loving heart is looking for people who will believe His Word and speak what He speaks, so we are in agreement with Him, not relying on our own thoughts. God specifically teaches us in the book of Proverbs 3:5-8 (AMP) to not lean on our own understanding, but instead we are supposed to trust in, rely on, and be confident in Him. *DOING this will be HEALTH to our bodies!* (see also Proverbs 4:20-22).

God is looking for people who will believe His Word and speak what He speaks, so we are in agreement with Him, not relying on our own thoughts.

WE HAVE BEEN AUTHORIZED BY CHRIST to humbly and prayerfully use Jesus' Name, speaking the Word of God with our hearts full of faith and trust in Him. We are to copy the Lord's example in all things: even His authority, because He told us *He* authorizes us. The Centurion in the gospels had fully grasped this, understanding that Jesus' word had authority. The Centurion told Jesus to *speak the word only*, and he knew his servant would be healed. He understood that Jesus' words could literally travel through time and space and get something done because of His anointing! Jesus commended the Centurion's faith, saying He had not seen such faith in all of Israel (referring to His own people who *should* have known and understood who He was!).

I did my best to obey and copy His Word, and I saw His glory and mercy! **What God has done for me, He is more than willing to do for you.**

There is *much* to understand about God's Word, receiving healing, and the power of believing and praying **HIS anointed words** into what appears to be impossible circumstances, as illustrated in Ezekiel 37. God is powerful and He will do what He has set out to accomplish. *His Word and His will do not contradict one another.*

AS I CONTINUE TO LEARN and study God's Word and His faithfulness, I am reminded of a lovely woman in a Bible study group who has taken a stand on God's Word for healing. She is ever-learning and increasing in the ability to apply God's Word to a battle with cancer. She has personally seen God's faithfulness and had repeated victories over several years.

She and I were walking into the home of our host one evening for a Bible study and she told me excitedly, "The doctor says my tumors have shrunk and gotten smaller!" I gave her a big hug and told her that was wonderful... even though her words felt like a kick in my spirit. (I knew that "kick" was to get my attention on her behalf for later that evening.)

I waited through the evening until a moment would come up when I could point out to her to not verbally "own" those cancerous tumors as *hers* by calling them *"my* tumors*"*. (The devil is in the details in looking for ways to *snipe* at us. Accidental words of death are like bullets that are licensed to be used against us!)

Returning to Ezekiel 37 for a moment, even thousands of years ago, while displaying His immeasurable and astonishing power to DO what *we* label "impossible", God was determined to get the lesson across to a man **"Speak MY WORDS" and watch what happens!"** *This is a theme with God,* not a modern-day fad or movement.

God is trying to get across to a man "Speak MY WORDS" and watch what happens!" This is a theme with God, not a modern-day fad or movement.

Ephesians 5:1 tells us to be imitators of God the same way a little child imitates his parents. We want to be full of God's Word and how *He* thinks (Romans 12:2) so that it's as natural a habit as breathing to recognize and catch words and thoughts that don't match *God's* ways of thinking.

As His disciples, *we are instructed to DO exactly that*! We're told to literally capture thoughts that do not honor what God says, bringing them into obedience to Christ by obeying II Corinthians 10:5. **That wise discipline will *protect us*!** It will keep us from misusing our words.

God is a Word-God. He created everything with Words. Hebrews 11:3 says that "by faith we understand that the worlds were framed by the Word of God." We are made in His image and likeness (Genesis 1:26) and we are the only part of His creation blessed with the power of speech and cognitive reason. ***Words matter***, and apparently they are supposed to matter a lot more than we have realized, because they sure matter to our Heavenly Father!

Back to talking about when I was sharing with the woman and the Bible study group right after she had told me "my tumors have shrunk"...

I said, "Why not give God praise for the shrinking of the tumors and say instead, "THE tumors are shrinking by the power of God" rather than say "*My* tumors".

I told her the Holy Spirit was teaching me about details. I said, "I don't call anything 'mine' that I don't want to *be* mine if it doesn't match God's Word and His covenant for me." As soon as I said that to her, she could "see" it and got excited about the difference.

I don't call anything 'mine' that I don't want to be mine if it doesn't match God's Word and His covenant for me.

Moments later someone in the group said, "We just need to pray for her cancer to go into remission".

Wham! Up rose inside of me words I knew were led of the Lord: "**No! It is not *her* cancer! Jesus did not give it to her, so she doesn't have to have it.** Jesus paid dearly for her to have *healing*, and *protection* and *deliverance* from disease. It is not *her* cancer at all!"

Then another thought came up even more strongly in my spirit. I said, "In fact, *remission isn't good enough.* It falls very short of God's best. **Scripture does NOT say, "By His stripes ye shall go into remission"**, but rather, **"By His stripes ye were *healed*!"**

The thoughts kept coming and I said, "Praying for *remission* is actually *giving the cancer permission to stay*, and that is not acceptable!

"Remission is still giving the cancer *a place*, an opportunity to go dormant, which means it is being licensed to wake up and become alive and destructive again. NO! Jesus did not suffer for that. He suffered to provide us complete healing and wholeness if we dare to reach for it, receive it, and take it. He loves us too much to have us think that way. Receiving the full impact of His sacrifice glorifies and honors Him."

Jesus suffered to provide us complete healing and wholeness if we dare to reach for it, receive it, and take it.

Everyone in the room caught the idea of us being sure we were agreeing with God's Word and not accidentally watering it down with our perceptions. We got excited about what we were learning right there "live from Heaven" at that moment.

That was a room of people who love God's Word and are hungry to know God intimately. THE SPIRIT OF THE LORD WAS REVEALING HOW SUBTLE THE ENEMY IS in finding ways of depleting what we have faith for so we don't get the *whole* blessing of God. If Satan can steal from us in the tiniest of details, he will. If he can blindside us using our own words against us as his authorization to attack or undermine us, or hinder our prayers, he will.

Accidental words of death are like bullets that are licensed to be used against us! Jesus Himself warned us about careless words.

No wonder God said in Hosea 4:6, "My people are destroyed for *lack of knowledge*" (*not* because it is His will!)

Even back when the devil was tempting Eve he tried to undermine the power of God's Word in her life by planting doubt and saying *"Has* God said...?"

When we study the account in Genesis, it is interesting to note that Eve misquoted to the devil what God had said. *It would have been much better if she had been completely accurate in remembering what God had said,* and then been a do-er of His words, that's for sure!

That is why we need to prayerfully look into each healing verse and humbly ask,

> "God, please teach me what You are saying in this verse from *Your* perspective. Don't let me be religiously dense or dull. Open my understanding wide to receive Your bigness, Your greatness, Your power and provision! Please weed out every bit of unbelief that is in my thinking, whether I am aware of it or not."

This brings God honor and He *will* answer that prayer! We prayed over that woman that evening, and within another couple weeks the tumors that had been in her body were 100% gone! Notice how I said that. I did not say, "*her* tumors were gone." In our bi-monthly meetings we all agreed to continue to press in with faith and prayer to push far beyond just believing the cancer was in remission, but rather we were asking for it to be completely eradicated, never to return.

I shared with her how the Lord had taught me to address any possible cancer cells in my body as rebel cells. If they were trying to live in or have dominion in my body they had to go:

"Cancer cells, in the Name of Jesus, you may *not* use my body as a host for rebelling against the Lord who created me! I want all my cells to be in line with the Word of God. Cells, you hear and obey the Word of the One Who designed you - you multiply at the rate *He* commands. You stop multiplying rebelliously at your own pace, and instead you rebel cells shrink up, die at the root, and disappear, not taking any of my healthy cells with you."

God *can* and *is willing* to heal you too. What He has done for me, He will do for you.

God can and is willing to heal you too. What He has done for me, He will do for you.

I am reminded of another remarkable time I witnessed His mercy and amazing power in someone's life. I got to see Him fulfill Scripture right out of the book of Acts – I have nicknamed this account of His mighty hand "The Teddy Bear Incident."

The Teddy Bear Incident

Several years ago I prayed for a young woman I had met while ministering in a recovery center. When I saw her come into the center, she was demonstrating behavior that the doctors called insanity. (I asked God about it and my heart was impressed with the thought that she had lots of demons: that was why she was frothing at the mouth, shrieking, and thrashing about so much).

Doctors subdued her with drugs and restraining ties, etc. When I asked the staff about her, they said her family told them she had been like that for months, growing ever worse. It saddened me. I had never seen anything like that. She shrieked like a tortured animal.

I started to pray for her the first day she came in. Based on what I saw God do for people in the biblical accounts, *I knew if I was bold enough to ask,* the Lord would be willing to help her and set her free.

Following are the three sets of Scriptures I was trusting God to back up with His power to help her:

Matthew 14:35, 36, "When the men of that place recognized Him, they sent out into all the surrounding region, brought to Him all who were sick, and begged Him that they might touch the hem of His garment. As many as touched it were made perfectly well."

Acts 19:11, 12, "Now <u>God</u> worked **unusual** miracles by the hands of Paul, so that even handkerchiefs or aprons were brought from his body to the sick, and the diseases left them and the evil spirits went out of them."

Acts 5:14-16, "And believers were increasingly added to the Lord, multitudes of both men and women, so that they brought the sick out into the streets and laid them on beds and couches, that at least the shadow of Peter passing by might fall on some of them. Also a multitude gathered from the surrounding cities to Jerusalem, bringing sick people and those who were tormented by unclean spirits, and they were all healed."

God's goodness and willingness has not diminished over the generations!

I prayed for guidance about what to do for that girl. The idea came to me to bring a teddy bear I owned and then to get it into her hands, but to FIRST pray God's promises in those special verses into the stuffed bear!

By faith I laid my hands on the teddy bear, and **I asked and trusted for _God's_ anointing power for healing and deliverance to be transferred _into_ the fabric of the bear when I prayed over it according to His Word.** (I saw in the book of Acts that He had sent His anointing into cloths to be put on people, I knew the issue wasn't what type of cloth! The issue was His mercy and power!)

Some might think, but how could you _know_ if He would do that? Because Scripture tells me God is the same yesterday, today, and forever, so it was logical to assume He would help her too! Remember, when the man came to Him for help, Jesus said to him "_I am willing._" God's goodness and willingness has not faded over the generations!

I asked God to do what I saw Him do in the Scriptures. After I prayed over the teddy bear, I sneaked into her room, approaching her cautiously to give her the stuffed bear. She let out shrieks that almost made me jump out of my skin, grabbed it like a wild animal, and proceeded to spit on it and bite it, but she also held it tight. Quite honestly, it pretty much scared me!

Each day when I went to the facility, I watched her to see what God was going to do. No one could pry that bear out of her hands. She clung to it constantly! Hour by hour she became calmer, more peaceful, and within four days she was completely in her right mind. The doctors were astonished. I knew what I had witnessed was a demonstration of the faithfulness of God. I got to see more "Acts" of the Holy Spirit!

God actually took care of _both_ of us. I had never seen anything like what I was observing in that girl, and it made my hair stand up on the back of my neck! It was scary and I was completely inexperienced in praying for someone like that. That girl would have clawed at me or spit on me if I had tried to approach her with my Bible or to actually touch her and pray for her...and so I'm sure that's why God came up with the "**Teddy Bear Plan**".

It was a practical and unusual way to meet the need of the moment, so *He* could get in there and be gracious to deliver and heal her, and protect me at the same time! **Acts 19:11, 12 says <u>God</u> did *unusual* things by the hands of Paul**. He was equally willing to do something unusual by anointing the cloth of a stuffed toy to help a girl in a modern-day facility in answer to prayer!

The unshakeable fact from age to age is this: God is always willing to show Himself faithful to anyone who will dare to believe Him!

GOD KNEW she would grab onto that teddy bear and not let go! As she did, *He honored my prayer* for Him to pour His healing power into the stuffed bear. The whole time she held it God was transferring His mercy and power into her, dealing with all the things *He alone* had the wisdom to know about - things I would never have been able to even guess at! I watched Him deliver and set her free. Her family and the doctors were all stunned. God is ever faithful, full of compassion, and changes not. The unshakeable fact is this: from age to age, God is always willing to show Himself faithful to anyone who will dare to believe Him!

He is also very creative about it at times! It was a precious day to watch her happily leave the hospital sound and whole without any need for medications, peacefully restored to her loved ones. Truly, once again He had watched over His Word to prosper it whereunto it was sent (Isaiah 55:11).

Quick Scripture References – Chapter Eleven

Isaiah 55 ...come up higher to His ways...AMP
Ezekiel 37 amazing display of God's power...NKJV
Ezekiel 37:4 God tells a man "speak My words..."NKJV
John 1:1 ...with God, and the WORD was GOD...NKJV
Rev. 19:13 ...His Name is the WORD of GOD...NKJV
II Chronicles 16:9 God seeks...to be strong for...NKJV
Proverbs 3:5-8 ...lean on/trust in God...AMP
Proverbs 4:20-22 His Word...healing to our flesh NKJV
Ephesians 5:1 ...be imitators of God...NIV
Romans 12:2 be transformed...renew your mind NKJV
II Corinthians 10:5 capture thoughts, obey Word NKJV
Hebrews 11:3 ...worlds formed by His Word NKJV
Genesis 1:26 we are made in His likeness NKJV
Hosea 4:6 people destroyed...lack of knowledge NKJV
Matthew 14:35,36 touched hem...were healed NKJV
Acts 19:11,12 garments...anointing...healed...NKJV
Acts 5:14-16 ...God anoints a shadow! NKJV
Isaiah 55:11 He produces with His Word NKJV

CHAPTER 12

Designed to Be an Overcomer

*"...we are more than conquerors through Him who
loved us."*
Romans 8:37 (NKJV)

GOD DESIGNED US TO BE OVERCOMERS and
powerful, not victims of our own poor habits. Healing
can come through being corrected. None of us can
change or fix what we're not aware of. Scripture tells us
that God's Spirit is not only a Helper, but He is also a
Corrector, Counselor, Teacher, and Guide.

Sometimes we handicap ourselves with the attitude
that we will only be open to being corrected about what
we have defined as sin in our life, but we don't want to
be corrected or to have any *other* accountability to God.
He may surprise us with what He would like to address
first in our lives.

Perhaps there's a fear that eats at us deep down inside,
a pervasive anxiety that is secretly with us all the time.

Maybe we don't want to let God meddle in how we compulsively spend money, how we eat, if we do or don't exercise, etc. I know I have sure struggled in developing any consistency in these areas! Maybe we don't want to let Him meddle with what we pollute our hearts and minds with on television or on the internet, or if we've developed a nicotine habit or a gluttony habit, a drug habit or a drinking habit. Facing these things can make us uncomfortable. One thing I know though, those "nudges of correction" from God are never to put us down or condemn us. *He is not like that.* Those nudges coming to us are to protect us and help us, if we will listen.

I stated, "Maybe we don't want to *let* God meddle..." That indicates two things: (a) we are exercising our personal power to choose to be resistant and closed to being corrected, and (b) we are lacking the needed spirit of cooperation with which God can readily work.

Those nudges coming to us are to protect us and help us, if we will listen.

Jesus said in John 8:31, 32, "If you *abide in My Word*, you are My disciples indeed, and you shall know the truth, and the truth shall set you free." God's Spirit doesn't just want to lead us in *spiritual* truth and stop there. These truths are specifically designed to roll over into *every practical area* of our lives! How else are we going to walk in the abundant life and be fully alive, healthy, and blessed the way God intends?

In John 14:26, Jesus told us the Holy Spirit would teach us "*All* things" and bring to our recollection what Jesus taught and said. Scripture says to devote ourselves in wisdom and holiness to God spiritually, and we are *also* told to be pragmatic, walk in His wisdom, and even *yield our own bodies to Him*. I especially like Romans 12:1-3 as explained in the contemporary language of The MESSAGE Bible, "So here's what I want you to do, God helping you: Take your everyday, ordinary life — your sleeping, eating, going-to-work, and walking-around life — and place it before God as an offering. Embracing what God does for you is the best thing you can do for Him. Don't become so well-adjusted to your culture that you fit into it without even thinking. Instead, fix your attention on God. You'll be changed from the inside out. Readily recognize what He wants from you, and quickly respond to it. Unlike the culture around you, always dragging you down to its level of immaturity, God brings the best out of you, develops well-formed maturity in you."

If we break it down by meditating on it, paying attention to all the layers of what's being said, we will see how thorough it is. Notice the following:

It talks about *us* making a decision to participate with God in our daily lives. It's a decision of dedication to participate responsibly. A decision to be devoted, living each day as an offering of love to this wonderful God! It's a decision to know His Word and be well-pleasing to Him (which means lining myself up with *God's* thoughts and ways, letting all of my *contrary thoughts* go!). It's very practical. When I think about all He has done for me and provided for me, why wouldn't I want to live that way? Living this way would certainly bring real relational healing to many families.

He *also* wants us to grasp the wonder of our bodies as talked about in Psalm 139. It says that we are fearfully and wonderfully made. We are a wonder! *God wants us to understand the broad impact of His Word telling us that our bodies are His temple.* I was certainly guilty of falling very short of living in that wisdom because of the way I lived on sugary junk food. Obesity and diabetes (at least a high percentage of it) would dwindle considerably if we committed to DO what the Word tells us about our bodies!

Then it dawned on me to also ask to <u>want</u> to be set free so I would willingly and cooperatively walk in the power He was giving me.

When I decided to yield to the convictions about the chocolate and other seriously poor eating habits I had practiced for more than half my life, I prayed and asked God to really help me and set me free. Initially I asked for His help, which He gave me, but then I would always go *back* to the bad habits.

Then it dawned on me to also ask to *want* to be set free so I would willingly and cooperatively walk in the power He was giving me. A verse came to mind that was *so specific* I was amazed! In Proverbs 23:1-3 it says, "When you sit down to eat with a ruler, consider carefully what is before you, and put a knife to your throat if you are a man given to appetite, do not desire his delicacies, for they are *deceptive food.*" BAM! Was that ever making it clear to me – chocolate is surely a deceptive food!

This shows just how specific and detailed God will be in applying Psalm 107:20 in our lives: "He sent His Word and He healed them." There is no detail into which He does not want to bring HIS HEALING HAND *and healing wisdom* to set us free!

For me, it was going to have to be my eating habits. In my case, eating enormous amounts of chocolate over many years took a toll in my body, and since finding out about a mass in my kidney, I have had to rethink how I ate all those years.

There is no detail into which He does not want to bring HIS HEALING HAND to set us free!

My consumption of chocolate was so ridiculous, if I didn't get my daily "fix", my hands would tremble like an alcoholic needing a drink! Yes, seriously! Seeking God for strength to overcome a true chocolate addiction, I began to also understand all the *psychological ways* I was addicted to chocolate - going all the way back to childhood and family traditions.

Some people might say, "Why would God let you get a mass in your kidney if He's so good?" Well, I need to be completely honest here and admit to how many times I got "nudges" quietly inside myself to stop eating so poorly.

I got those nudges repeatedly for *years* prior to getting that tumor and being told I had cancer. I just had not been willing to heed them and change!

God was trying to HEAL ME PREVENTATIVELY AND PROTECTIVELY, but I wouldn't listen! I knew it was Wisdom calling to me, but I didn't want to tie it to God. I didn't listen, preferring to ignore those nudges so I could continue to indulge myself. Ouch! Have you been getting nudges about anything that you choose to ignore?

If that is the case, my guess is *God has already been trying to watch out for you for a long time* and He's trying to spare you something down the road. Will you take heed and follow His lead, letting HIS WISDOM be a *preventative healing* to you?

Have you been getting nudges about anything that you choose to ignore?

I was discovering that when we approach God for healing, He may pursue healing us even more thoroughly than we had ever originally hoped for or anticipated! He goes after the *root* of the issue if we let Him. He wants us to know the truth so we can be set free. *He is intimately detailed in His love for us*, and since each one of us is unique, we will discover just how personal He will get in talking to us about the truth, so He can keep His Word to us, really set us free, and heal us.

He is a good Papa! Maybe some of you didn't have that kind of an earthly dad in your family growing up, so it's a challenge for you to grasp that God would love you that thoroughly. Yes, He would, and He does. He loves YOU that dearly; you matter to Him!

There may be crucial unresolved issues that are at the root of the problem. If we allow ourselves to start a habit that is drug related (whether illegal drugs, prescriptions, nicotine, or alcohol), it's important we don't borrow the labels society now gives it, and call it a disease. Doing that allows us to psychologically play the "helpless" card.

God will help us, because He does not deal in excuses; He deals in truth, power, provision and results!

The danger of labeling certain things "disease" is it can water-down the way God would like us to see it. He is powerful, and He wants *us* to be powerful as well, not "excuse-full".

If we allowed those bad habits, we will begin to get our power back by getting honest with ourselves and putting the responsibility where it belongs – on us. To be set free and to get healed, we need to *own* the issue, whatever that issue might be. For me, it was the daily addiction of poisoning myself with absurd amounts of chocolate and sugar!

If we face the truth that *we* started doing something one day, which led us to where we are now, that's the first step to get free. God will help us, because **He does not deal in excuses; He deals in truth**, in power, provision and results!

God not only wants to liberate us from whatever our habit is, He also wants to deal with and heal the root weakness. That involves *us* being willing (and having the courage) to have an honest heart before Him – **the help and strength is there for the asking**.

At the heart of most of our weakness and sin is rebellion and disrespect. Disrespect for what we know is right or best, and an I-don't-care,-I-want-my-way-right-now attitude. Some of us don't even know how to respect *ourselves*!

We may have a propensity for being particularly weak in a certain area, perhaps even with a DNA weakness, but God doesn't want to leave us weak, and He doesn't want to leave us diseased. So, let's ask for help and not make excuses. Also, He is Lord over DNA. We do not have to play helpless and settle with the excuse of "Well, I inherited this from my mother or my father." Scripture says we have inherited *ALL* things *new* if we have received Christ personally as Lord of our lives.

In 2 Corinthians 5:17 (NLT) it says, "...those who become Christians become new persons. They are not the same anymore, for the old life is gone. A new life has begun!"

The Lord is letting us know He has the power to make everything about us new - more than we realize. That's why we need to pursue getting our minds transformed to how He wants us to think, so we can continually be in an ever-increasing state of fully inheriting all He has for us. He has HEALING FOR US in many more ways than the obvious ones we tend to focus on!

Even Alcoholics Anonymous teaches people to own the issue, and to seek a Higher Power to get strength to become a victor, rather than remain a victim. That too, is part of the healing process. We get to remind ourselves that page upon page in the Bible, God tells us we are loved and He is merciful, so that is a real confidence-booster to know WE CAN COME TO HIM FOR HELP AND HEALING ABOUT *ANY*THING!

He has HEALING FOR US in many more ways than the obvious ones we tend to focus on!

Quick Scripture References – Chapter Twelve

John 8:31, 32   If you abide in My Word…NKJV
John 14:26   Holy Spirit will teach us all things…NKJV
Rom. 12:1   dedicate our bodies…as sacrificial service…MSSG
Psalm 139   we are fearfully and wonderfully made…NKJV
Proverbs 23:1-3   deceptive food…NKJV
Psalm 107:20   He sent His Word and healed them…NKJV
2 Corinthians 5:17   made new creation in Christ…NLT

*   *   *

CHAPTER 13

He Will Hear Your Prayers

(Prayers for Healing and Salvation)

"You are forgiving and good, O Lord,
abounding in love to all who call to you."
Psalm 86:5 (NIV)

Praying for Your Healing

We must learn how to pray for healing! This is not a fad, a game, or a formula. Come to God in childlike faith, trusting *His* "bigness" and *His* goodness. Study and believe His promises about healing. Study Jesus in the gospels and His healing mercy. *Study God's healing covenant Scriptures until you KNOW they are for you.*

The Bible teaches that faith will come. How? By hearing the Word of God. Be willing to repent of sin. Repent does not just mean *confess* sin, as in a church confessional, admitting guilt. That is the first step, but it's *more* than that. "Repent!" was Jesus' first message, and it means to *turn away* from sin and disobedience with a determination to go in a new direction, *God's* direction. It is far more than a New Year's resolution to 'do better'. *It cannot be accomplished apart from Him.*

If you haven't asked Christ into your heart and yielded your life to Him, do that first and foremost. What could be better than to have The Healer take up residence in your own heart? You can begin by using the promises shared in this book. Then search the Scriptures and find other promises you are trusting God for, bring them to Him, and pray His Word. For example:

"Heavenly Father, I see in Your Word that You are merciful and willing to heal. Your Word let's me know I can come to Your throne of grace boldly and with confidence, to find help in time of need. I come to You in the Name of Your Son Jesus Christ, who tells me I can ask You anything in His Name. (Fill in the blank by naming your need to God) _____ is going on in my body, and I need Your healing touch. Your Word tells me I was healed by the stripes of Jesus and You spoke that as an established fact 700 years before Jesus was even born in a body to take that beating for me! Based on Your Word, Lord, I come to you in faith, nothing wavering, asking You to manifest in my body the healing You have already provided for me through the beating Jesus took for me.

"Thank You for Your mercy, thank You for loving me, and thank You for meeting my need with Your power and promise. Thank You Jesus for Your great sacrifice to seal and fulfill the covenant of healing which God has established for me by His promises. I will continue to feed on Your Word and put it into myself like a medicine, trusting You to watch over Your Word to produce healing in me. Thank You that You per*fect* those things which concern me. I love You Lord, in Jesus' Name, Amen."

This prayer is based on the following Scriptures which I am listing, so you know you are praying God's Word, and therefore you can be confident you ARE praying *His will:*

Hebrews 4:14-16, Isaiah 53:5, James 1:5-7, Isaiah 53:3,6,7, and 11, and also Psalm 138 (the entire Psalm), Proverbs 4:20-22

Once you have prayed, if your *feelings* go up or down, or tell you He will not heal you, or His Word isn't powerful, you remind yourself of *His* character, *His* stability, *His* unfailing love, and what He did for me and my kidney, and what He did for that girl I gave that teddy bear to. Remember, be tenacious like the Canaanite woman (Matthew 15:22-28) I mentioned earlier. Jesus taught people to keep asking, she *did*, and look what happened for her!

My hope and prayer in writing this book and sharing these accounts is to assist you in being securely anchored in the Scriptures and God's goodness concerning healing. I hope that any previously held doubts will melt away as the truth is known and you are set free from unbelief.

My prayer is that you will be encouraged and strengthened to say, *"As for me, I will choose to cling to the Word of God every time"* when it comes to healing (or anything else!). I trust this will also create a wonderful ripple effect into all other areas of your life, as well.

Receiving Jesus Personally Into Your Own Life

If you believe Jesus to be God's Son, but didn't previously have these perspectives about Him and the Word of God, talk to Him about these things now. Tell Him how awesome it is to discover He is so good! Tell Him you want to know Him in all the wonderful ways that *He* wants you to know Him.

Tell Him you don't want to be limited to your own perspectives anymore, but you want to become filled with an understanding of how *He* thinks and what *His* perspectives are!

ASK for an ever-increasing appetite and love for His Word, the Scriptures, so that you can walk and live daily in Romans 12:2 through the leadership of His Holy Spirit. Jesus told us in the gospels to "...ask, and keep on asking."

ASK for the Holy Spirit: He is God's Spirit, full of wisdom and light, power and grace. Ask Him to engulf you in His love, to help you pursue studying God's Word, and to give you understanding as you do, thereby enabling you to better and more intimately know Him.

When I was nineteen years old I believed in God, and I knew the account of what I called "the Christmas story" and "the Easter story", but knowing an account of something versus *personally* knowing the Lord Jesus *Himself* is vastly different.

I was invited to a Jesus rock-concert with some friends in my second year of college. When the music stopped playing, a long-haired kid with a giant wad of gum in his mouth stood up on an orange crate (no kidding) on a gymnasium floor at Wilson High School in Long Beach,

California. He talked about knowing Jesus in an intimate way. He said if I asked Him to, Jesus would literally come live inside my heart and take up permanent residence there! He also said that Christ would make me clean and new, and teach me how to walk side-by-side with Him every day. I had never heard anything like that in my life up until that point, even though I had faithfully attended church for many years, sung in the choir, etc. I responded by getting out of my seat to go forward for prayer as fast as I could. I dropped to my knees to pray. I didn't hear much of what that kid said after that, but I opened my mouth and on my own prayed something like this:

> "Jesus, I've always sort of believed in You, but I never knew You would come live inside my heart literally and wash away my sin completely, making me new and clean. I never knew You would *come live inside me and teach me to know Your voice, love Your Word, and have a super personal relationship with You.* My goodness! *I WANT that! DO it!*
>
> "I want to know You, not only as Savior, but I want to have You be Lord, in charge, the Captain of my life. I BELIEVE You are God's Son, and that You died on the cross for me personally, so I can belong to God and not be condemned for my sins. I believe You rose from the dead. Come into my heart and own me, make me Yours - and I want You to be mine! I know I need to be made clean from sin, I know I need power from the Holy Spirit to live for You the way this kid is talking about!"

The Lord has faithfully kept me in His loving hand ever since I prayed that prayer. *There have been times when I was far less than true to Him, but He has always remained constant in Himself, true to His Word, and true to me.* He is *always* willing to draw me close to His heart when I approach Him in prayer.

As I get older, I'm learning the smart place to be is to "stick and stay" close to His side! I stay close to Him by keeping myself in His Word, so that I can hear His Spirit whisper into my heart, to love me, protect me, guide me, instruct me, correct me, and encourage or warn me.

Some days I "feel" like doing this; honestly, however, there are plenty of days I don't feel like it, but I do it anyway. It is a discipline, the same as working out at the gym or eating healthfully, but the dividends are beyond this planet!

If you are someone who has never prayed and asked Jesus Christ to be your Savior and Lord, please do so now! If you want to know you are saved, and to know Jesus personally for yourself, just open your heart and your mouth and ask as I did.

Be real with Him, be yourself, and be sure you are willing to repent (turn away from sin) and that you really *want* a new life with Him as your Lord (to be Captain of your ship, giving your life over to Him).

You can borrow the words I used (I put them in italics, as you can see) if they are close to what you mean in your own heart, or just say your own words. There is no set "right or wrong wording" per se - that is not the issue; it is what is in your heart that matters...

*"Lord God, please wash away my sin
completely with Your holiness, and please
come live inside my heart, making me new and
clean. Please forgive me of all my sin. Come
live in the center of my heart and teach me to
know Your voice, love Your Word, and have a
personal relationship with You. I WANT that!
DO it!*

*"Jesus, I receive you as my Savior. I yield to
you as Lord, the Captain of my life. I BELIEVE
You are God's Son, and that You died on the
cross for me personally, so I can belong to
God and not be condemned for my sins. I
believe You rose from the dead, conquering
death and sin forever! Take over in my life,
make me Yours - and I want YOU to be mine! I
trust You to make me new and clean from sin. I
ask for power from the Holy Spirit to live for
You. Fill me with Your Spirit, Lord. I pray in
Your Name Jesus, and I thank You for
answering my prayer."*

God is looking on your heart -- He sees you, knows
your name, and treasures you. He loves you - *He wants
your heart and your loyalty.*

Salvation and the opportunity to belong to Jesus Christ
and know Him are as close to you as your own breath, in
this very moment! God even explains the moment you
are in right now, and He makes it crystal clear for us in
Romans 10: 8-11, which says, "But what does it say?
'The word is near you, in your mouth and in your heart'
(that is, the word of faith which we preach): that if you

153

confess with your mouth the Lord Jesus and believe in your heart that God has raised Him from the dead, you will be saved. For with the heart one believes unto righteousness, and with the mouth confession is made unto salvation. For the Scripture says, 'Whoever believes on Him will not be put to shame.'"

Romans 9:33 also says, "...the one who trusts in Him will never be put to shame." (NIV)

You have been learning about the Word of God and receiving it into your heart. The Holy Spirit of God causes it to become "quickened" like an "aha" moment and wants you to decide to respond to His love for you right here and now. You can acknowledge that you are indeed a sinner with no hope of being perfect or righteous *on your own* and that you need Him. (Way deep down inside we all know that about ourselves). Jesus bore the pressure of being perfect *for* you, and God credits His righteousness *to you* as an amazing gift of LOVE.

This is set into motion with your mouth and heart by agreeing with what He is telling you in His Word!

• He wants you to recognize He is far greater and wiser than you are;

• It would be foolish to not yield to His goodness and love!

• He enters your heart when you *invite* Him to. How amazing that our Creator so respects the free will *HE* gave us, He waits until we use it to invite Him into our hearts before He comes in! He doesn't crash in, boss us around, and grab our will from us.

He lets us keep it, and learn by choice to yield and align it to His wisdom and love.

• We bring the gift of free will, which He gave us, and lay it at His feet like a badge of honor between Him and us.

• It becomes a partnership of love. We are responding with the very will He gave us; we are freely bringing our hearts and lives *in response* to the great love *He* is offering.

• From then on, when we pray, He looks on our hearts and sees His own Son's face looking back at Him. It's remarkable! It is because of Jesus' sacrifice on the cross that we are made wholly acceptable to the Father. The Bible even says that Jesus presents us to God **blameless**! Jesus is actually called our Advocate and High Priest before God! (Please read Hebrews 4:14-16)

The Creator is reaching out to each individual one of us with His own nail-scarred hand and saying, "Be Mine!" How could we resist such a One who loves us so completely?! It is the greatest love story of all time!

He guarantees this as real and unshakeable because, thankfully, it is a transaction that is *not* based on the unpredictability of how we *feel*, but rather is based on *His* unchanging character and *His* Word.

When you pray and do this, He seals you unto His own heart. From that point forward, when the Heavenly Father looks on you any time you pray, He sees you wrapped up IN Jesus. Christ Himself has taken up

residency within your heart *because you asked Him to.*
Only God could think of something this clever!

Thank goodness salvation is based on *Him*, rather than
us! We don't have to bear the weight of being good
enough to be saved, because He was good enough *for* us.

**If you have prayed just now and done this, I would
like to give you an illustration of how secured you
have just become**. Do this with me: If you have a ring,
take it off your finger and hold it in your hand. *The ring
represents you*. Now, take the ring and put it in your
strongest hand, and close your hand around the ring in a
tight fist. Done that? That tightly-clasped, fisted hand
securely wrapped around the ring represents Christ Jesus
wrapped around you. Then, take your other free hand
and clasp it around the hand that is *already* tightly
holding the ring, making a new fist around the first fist.
That second outer fisted hand represents the Heavenly
Father! Will that ring (you) get dropped or lost? Nope, I
don't think so! It is secured *by that which holds it*, and
you are secured by Who is holding you in His loving
grip. You never need to fear death; you are safe in Him.

Welcome to the Family of God! You have a wonderful
promise (one of thousands which you have inherited
through Christ) from Him in John 1:12, "But to as many
as did receive and welcome Him, He gave the authority
(power, privilege, and right) to become the children of
God..." (AMP). That is talking about *you* and what has
just transpired if you prayed the prayer to receive Christ.

God is not going to change His mind about you. He
paid with the Life of His own Son to come after you and
pursue you with His love!

Get yourself a Bible (the New King James Version, or the New International Version are good for beginners) that is translated into modern-day language, and read it daily. Some churches will provide a Bible as a gift. Start in the gospel of John in the New Testament, read a chapter (or more) a day, and read it *out loud* and carefully, because it says in Scripture faith comes by *hearing* the Word of God. Discover all that you have inherited!

When you have questions, ask God to help you understand. Put a little date in the margin of your Bible where you had the question. He will get answers to your understanding.

Read the New Testament thoroughly a few times through. Wonderful places to read in the Old Testament are the Psalms, the Proverbs, Deuteronomy, and Isaiah; these are some of my favorites! The Proverbs are full of very practical "one liner" wisdom thoughts for daily living.

The more you read God's Word, the more the ability to sense His guidance will develop within you. Jesus said, "My sheep know my voice, and the voice of a stranger they will not follow." This is the beginning of the most amazing relationship of your life. Nurture it. *Make it your utmost priority!*

Find a good church where the whole good news of God's love and Word is taught so you can grow in faith (not in doubt!).

If you would care to write to me and tell me you have prayed to receive Jesus or have received healing, I would be thrilled to hear from you and pray for you.

Quick Scripture References – Chapter Thirteen

Hebrews 4:14-16 Jesus is our Advocate of Mercy NKJV
Isaiah 53:5 …we are healed by His stripes…NKJV
James 1:5-7 …come to God in faith, not doubt NKJV
Isaiah 53:3,6,7, and 11 Prophecies of Messiah NKJV
Psalm 138 An amazing Psalm revealing God NKJV
Proverbs 4:20-22 His Word is health, healing NKJV
Matthew 15:22-28 the feisty Canaanite woman's faith…NIV

Romans 12:2 be transformed, renew your mind NKJV
Romans 10:8-11 HOW TO GET SAVED… NKJV
Romans 9:33 trust in Christ…never put to shame…NIV
Hebrews 4:14-16 Jesus is our Advocate NKJV

Closing Thoughts From The Word

"Lord, if you are willing, you can make me clean..."
"I am willing," He said.
Matthew 8:2, 3 (NIV)

"Yet for us there is [only] one God, the Father,
Who is the Source of all things and for Whom we [have
life], and one Lord, Jesus Christ, through and by
Whom are all things, and through and by Whom we
[ourselves exist]."
1 Corinthians 8:6 (AMP)

"Now to Him who is able to do immeasurably more
than all we ask or imagine,
according to His power that is at work within us,
to Him be glory...throughout all generations,
forever and ever! Amen."
Ephesians 3:20-21 (NIV)

Thoughts for Wisdom and Encouragement

There is an old saying: "Faith prays, and love gives the medicine". Jackie's story of faith reflects her own responsible pursuit of medical assistance, diagnosis, and follow-through to a needed surgery, while actively pursuing the revealed power of God in His Word, fully expecting Him to be her Healer.

If anyone believes they are sick and needs a doctor, no part of this story in any way suggests that a person should not then make the intelligent and responsible choice to see their doctor or seek medical assistance on behalf of themselves, their children, or other family members.

The intention of this book is clear in its introduction. It was written to encourage faith and hope in those who read it, in whatever situation they may find themselves – to equip people to better understand that God is very approachable and loves them more than they realize! He is still real and powerful today in very practical ways. He is Almighty, and is willing to meet them where they are, with open arms. Jesus Christ is available to all peoples, of all nations and backgrounds, and will not turn anyone away who comes to Him with a desire to know Him personally. He is Savior, He will be Friend, and yes, *He still heals today*. In the gospels, a man with leprosy came to Him saying, "Lord, if you are willing, you are able to cure me and make me clean." Jesus' answer to the man who approached Him for help still stands today for each of us: "I AM WILLING".

There is tremendous power in the Scriptures. Jackie sincerely hopes to stir a desire in others to pursue God and His Word for themselves. He is the Lord Who Heals.

BIOGRAPHY

Jacquelin Priestley has a passion for encouraging people to trust God for healing, and to share with them about *the power that resides within the Scriptures themselves*. They are alive, God-breathed, and full of His Life and Light. (II Timothy 3:16 and John 1:4)

She gave her life to Christ during her first year in college, while pursuing a degree in speech and communications. In 1993 she felt led to return to school to pursue a degree in Biblical Studies. She has served the Lord for over 20 years at Cottonwood Church in Los Alamitos, California, in music ministry, convalescent team ministries, and on a Romania missions team.

Jacquelin experienced the Lord's healing power in her own body for the first time after telling others about Jesus as Healer for several years. God's Word prospered within her as she gave it out to others. She has had many opportunities to pray for people and see God's faithfulness to honor His Name and His Word and bring healing.

Her message is enthusiastic, and unwavering – Jesus is Lord, He is the Living Word of God; His Word is alive and powerful, and God is still the Lord Our God Who Heals us!

If you would like to order more books, please contact us at www.HisWordHealedMe.com. You may write Jacquelin at:

JP@HisWordHealedMe.com
or

His Word Healed Me
PO Box 6393
Garden Grove, California 92846

SCRIPTURE REFERENCE LIST

Chapter 1

Psalm 56:3 …when afraid, will trust in Thee   KJV
Psalm 30:1-4 I cried to You, You have healed me AMP
Isaiah 53:1 Who will believe the report of the Lord? NKJV
Isaiah 59:19 Spirit raised up a standard…NKJV
II Timothy 3:15, 16 Every Scripture God-breathed AMP
Hebrews 13:5 God will never leave or forsake us AMP
Exodus 15:26 God is the Lord Who heals me   AMP
Psalm 30:3 …You have kept me alive… AMP
Isaiah 26:3 …perfect peace…fix mind on God…KJV
III John 2 …prosper, be in health as your soul prospers NKJV
Proverbs 4: 20-22 …His Word is health and healing   AMP

Chapter 2

James 5:14 …anoint with oil, get prayer from elders NKJV
James 5:16 …confess your sins that you may be healed NIV
James 5:15 …if sick have sinned, will be forgiven NIV
Isaiah 53:5 …healed by the stripes of Jesus NKJV
Exodus 15:26b …He is the Lord God Who heals us NKJV
Matthew 12:36, 37 …will be judged for our careless words NIV
I John 1:9 God is faithful to forgive us and cleanse us   NKJV
I John 1:8 …don't deny being a sinner…self-deceived…NKJV
Isaiah 26:3 …perfect peace…mind fixed on God… NLT
Isaiah 9:6 …a Child is born…Mighty God…   NKJV
Matthew 1:23 …and you shall call His name Jesus…NKJV
Matthew 12:34 …out of …heart the mouth will speak…NKJV
James 1:6, 7 …don't be double-minded…can't receive NIV
Joshua 1:6-9 …don't let His Word depart from mouth…NKJV
Deut. 6:1-9 remembering His Word causes good success NKJV
Isaiah 53:5 …by His stripes we are healed….NKJV
Psalm 107:20 …He sent His Word and healed them…NKJV
Hebrews 4:12 God's Word is alive and powerful…   AMP

Hebrews 13:8   Jesus the same yesterday, today, forever…NIV
Isaiah 53:1-5   What God accomplished through Messiah NKJV
Nehemiah 8:10   … joy of the Lord is your strength…NKJV
Psalm 16:11   …In His presence is fullness of joy…NKJV
Isaiah 55: 9-13   …God produces with His Word…NKJV
Romans 10:17   Faith comes by hearing…the Word…NKJV
Psalm 103:1-5   Bless the Lord, remember His benefits NKJV

Chapter 3

James 5:16b   heartfelt prayer of a righteous man avails…AMP
Proverbs 4:23   keep my heart with all diligence…NKJV
II Corinth 10:4, 5 .. bring every thought into obedience…NKJV
Isaiah 54:17   No weapon formed against me…NASB
Proverbs 26:2   A curse without cause will not alight…NKJV
Proverbs 4:20-22   God's Word is health and healing…AMP
Isaiah 40:8   God's Word stands forever…AMP
Mark 13:31   Jesus' Words will never pass away…NKJV
Psalm 103:1-5   …forget not all His benefits…NKJV
John 1:1   …the Word was with God….and was God NKJV
John 1:14 …Word became flesh, and dwelt among us…NKJV
II Timothy 1:7   …not given fear…but a sound mind…AMP
Hebrews 13:5   I will never leave you nor forsake you…NKJV
Isaiah 43:2   tough or scary times, God will help, protect…KJV
Isaiah 26:3   perfect peace if keep mind on the Lord…KJV
Phillip. 2:9-11   Name above every name…NASB
Mark 11:23   say to the mountain, don't doubt in heart…NKJV
Matthew 7:24-26   hear and DO His teachings…NKJV
James 1:22-25   DO the word, not just hear it…NKJV

Chapter 4

Isaiah 53:3-5   healed by his stripes…AMP
I Corinthians 1:30   Christ made unto us wisdom…KJV

Chapter 5

Isaiah 54:17   No weapon formed against you...NKJV
Matthew 4:1-11   Jesus uses Scripture to resist the devil!...AMP
Isaiah 53:5   Healed by His stripes...NKJV
Hebrews 4:12   The Word is alive and powerful...AMP
Isaiah 55:11 ...His Word will not return to Him void ...NKJV
Psalm 30:2-3   I cried to You and You have healed me...AMP
Isaiah 53:1   God asks: Who has believed Our report...NKJV
Proverbs 6:22   God's Word will speak *with* you...NKJV
John 1:1, 4, and 14   In the beginning was the Word...NKJV
John 1:4   ...in Him is Light...He is the Light of men...NKJV

Chapter 6

Isaiah 53:5   by His scourging we are healed...NKJV
Isaiah 52:14   His appearance was marred...NIV
Psalm 107:20   He sent His Word and healed them...NKJV

Chapter 7

None listed in this chapter.

Chapter 8

None listed in this chapter.

Chapter 9

Matthew 13:58 unbelief of the people hindered Jesus...NKJV
James 1: 6, 7 have faith, don't waiver or won't receive...NIV
Hosea 4:6 Lack of knowledge destroys *God's* people...NKJV
Isaiah 55:11 His Word will produce whereunto it's sent...NKJV

Chapter 10

Isaiah 54:17   No weapon formed against me will prosper   NIV
Isaiah 54:14, 15   ...terror shall be far from me...NIV
Isaiah 55:11   His Word produces wherein it is sent ...NKJV

Chapter 11

Isaiah 55   ...come up higher to His ways...AMP
Ezekiel 37   amazing display of God's power...NKJV
Ezekiel 37:4   God tells a man "speak My words"   NKJV
John 1:1   ...with God, and the WORD was GOD...NKJV
Rev. 19:13   ...His Name is the WORD of GOD...NKJV
II Chronicles 16:9   God seeks...to be strong for...NKJV
Proverbs 3:5-8   ...lean on/trust in God...AMP
Proverbs 4:20-22 His Word...healing to our flesh NKJV
Ephesians 5:1   ...be imitators of God...NIV
Romans 12:2   be transformed...renew your mind   NKJV
II Corinthians 10:5   capture thoughts, obey Word NKJV
Hebrews 11:3   ...worlds formed by His Word   NKJV
Genesis 1:26   we are made in His likeness   NKJV
Hosea 4:6   people destroyed...lack of knowledge   NKJV
Matthew 14:35,36   touched hem...were healed   NKJV
Acts 19:11,12   garments...anointing...healed...NKJV
Acts 5:14-16   ...God anoints a shadow!   NKJV
Isaiah 55:11   He produces with His Word   NKJV

Chapter 12

John 8:31, 32   If you abide in My Word...NKJV
John 14:26   Holy Spirit will teach us all things...NKJV
Rom. 12:1   dedicate our bodies...as sacrificial service...MSSG
Psalm 139   we are fearfully and wonderfully made...NKJV
Proverbs 23:1-3   deceptive food...NKJV

Psalm 107:20   He sent His Word and healed them...NKJV
2 Corinthians 5:17   made new creation in Christ...NLT

Chapter 13

Hebrews 4:14-16 Jesus is our Advocate of Mercy NKJV
Isaiah 53:5 ...we are healed by His stripes...NKJV
James 1:5-7 ...come to God in faith, not doubt NKJV
Isaiah 53:3,6,7, and 11 Prophecies of Messiah NKJV
Psalm 138 An amazing Psalm revealing God NKJV
Proverbs 4:20-22 His Word is health, healing NKJV
Matthew 15:22-28 the feisty Canaanite woman's faith...NIV
Romans 12:2 be transformed, renew your mind NKJV
Romans 10:8-11 HOW TO GET SAVED... NKJV
Romans 9:33 trust in Christ...never put to shame...NIV
Hebrews 4:14-16 Jesus is our Advocate NKJV

Ordering Information

His Word Healed Me can be ordered directly from the website: www.HisWordHealedMe.com.

Speaking and Teaching Engagements

It would be wonderful to hear from you if the book has impacted you, you've received healing, or received Jesus as your personal Savior! You may write to:

His Word Healed Me
P.O. Box 6393
Garden Grove, CA 92845

To request scheduling for Jacquelin to come share her story, teach and minister, please email her at:

JP@HisWordHealedMe.com
or call
1-866-777-9396

For the AUDIO version of the book, download on:
http://www.cdbaby.com/cd/jacquelinpriestley

Also available on KINDLE

May the Lord's grace and healing unfold in your life as you read!

Jacquelin Priestley

Made in the USA
San Bernardino, CA
12 November 2018